The Golden Rule of Leadership

The Golden Rule of Leadership

Richard L. Aude

iUniverse, Inc.
New York Lincoln Shanghai

The Golden Rule of Leadership

iUniverse books may be ordered through booksellers or by contacting:

iUniverse
2021 Pine Lake Road, Suite 100
Lincoln, NE 68512
www.iuniverse.com
1-800-Authors (1-800-288-4677)

ISBN-13: 978-0-595-33486-5 (pbk)
ISBN-13: 978-0-595-78288-8 (cloth)
ISBN-13: 978-0-595-78282-6 (ebk)
ISBN-10: 0-595-33486-5 (pbk)
ISBN-10: 0-595-78288-4 (cloth)
ISBN-10: 0-595-78282-5 (ebk)

Printed in the United States of America

For Mary, Madison & McKenzie

Contents

The Secret of Leadership

The only way to have a friend is to be one.

Ralph Waldo Emerson

Harry Truman once said, "The only new history is the history we've forgotten." The same could be said for leadership. Everything we need to know about the fundamental nature of leadership has been known for more than three thousand years. Yet, as of this writing, Amazon.com alone lists 9,658 books under the topic of leadership. Why is that? And what are the implications?

Well, perhaps more than anything else, it says—as Harry Truman suggested—we may have forgotten, or at least stopped paying attention to what we already know. But, such a large volume of books also says that almost anything can be construed as falling under the leadership umbrella. I'm sure there are numerous overlapping topics and theories in those 9,000-plus books. But I'm equally sure there are an enormous number of unique ideas and thoughts.

This poses a real challenge for those who are interested in learning more about leadership, or who want to enhance their leadership capabilities. The challenge is, how do you choose? Which book, or books, do you read? Whose theories do you choose to adopt? Which frameworks and methodologies are "right" for you? How do you sort through all of this information?

The answer, of course, is—you don't. It's literally impossible. Even if you were able to read a book a day (a task that most would agree is impossible), it would take more than twenty-six years just to read all the books currently in print.

So, what most people do is check the business bestseller lists to see what everybody else is reading, the theory being, I suppose, that all those people can't be wrong. Therefore, given that strategy, what you read (and, therefore, I suspect, attempt to adopt as your leadership approach) depends on when you decide to begin your leadership enhancement journey. The current gurus are Larry Bossidy and Rudi Guiliani. Last year it was Jack Welch. The year before, Bill Gates. Back in the eighties, it was Lee Iacocca. Who knows who it will be next year?

So, you choose your guru, you read the book, and you diligently attempt to apply what you've learned. What happens? Well, some people can apply the lessons, and some people can't. For those who are able to apply the lessons, some can make them work, and some can't. For those who are able to make them work, they're successful sometimes, and sometimes they're not.

Why is that? The answer is straightforward and obvious, yet, at the same time, amazingly difficult to see. The reason it's so incredibly difficult to successfully apply the lessons of these great leaders is because there's only one Rudi Guiliani. There's only one Larry Bossidy. There's only one Jack Welch, and so on. What works for them works for them because of their upbringing, education, and experiences. Because of the organizations they've been a part of. Because of the situations they've faced. Because of who they are.

All those things are very different, not only for the rest of us, but for each of them as well. You simply cannot "adopt" someone else's background, education and experiences. You must deal with your own. And, since your life experiences are different from theirs, your leadership lessons and needs will be different. It might very well be as difficult for Rudi Guiliani to successfully apply Jack Welch's lessons as it would be for you or me to do so.

So what do you do? That's where consultants and academicians in the field of leadership can provide a valuable service. They take the lessons of leaders like Guiliani, Bossidy, Welch, Iacocca et al., generalize them and build frameworks and methodologies to help the rest of us apply them.

And what happens? Well, some people can apply these generic frameworks and methodologies, and some people can't. Of those who can, sometimes they work, and sometimes they don't. And so on. History repeats itself.

When these lessons don't "stick," when better leaders are not emerging from the consulting process or educational program, the problem can only be one of three things: the consultant (or teacher), the student, or the "message."

If the problem is with the consultant/teacher, it's easily solved—simply dismiss that individual and bring in someone new. In the rough and tumble corporate world, there is little patience with ineffective teachers or consultants. Companies pay a lot of money for these services, and if someone isn't "cutting the mustard," that *someone* gets cut...and fast.

That leaves the student and the message. But how can it be the message? After all, if Jack Welch said it, how could it be wrong? Or if the prestigious XYZ Consulting Company is teaching it, it must be right. So the problem has to be with the student.

But all my instincts tell me the answer isn't that simple. On the one hand, it's too easy to just cavalierly dismiss people. And on the other, how could all these messages—these frameworks and methodologies—be wrong. Too many dedicated, talented people have worked too hard to develop them. So why don't they work—or at least why don't they work a lot more often? Why is there such a disconnect between theory and application?

The answer is actually pretty straightforward. The essence of leadership is not formulaic. It's not a methodology. Not a process. It's highly individual. There are as many styles of leadership as there are leaders. Hence the 9,658 books. And that takes us back to the title of this chapter—the surprising little secret of leadership: every one of us already knows everything we need to know about the fundamental nature of leadership. We've known it since we were children. Our parents taught it to us. And their parents taught it to them. And so on back through history for at least three thousand years.

The essence of effective leadership can be summed up in one simple, yet profound, statement: "Do unto others as you would have them do unto you." The Golden Rule. Expressed most often as shown in the previous sentence, but I think more usefully stated as "Treat other people the way you would like to be treated."

While this statement is perhaps most often attributed to Christ in his Sermon on the Mount, please don't misconstrue it as an exclusively Christian ethic. Virtually every major religion has expressed this sentiment in one form or another, and philosophers throughout the ages have articulated similar thoughts.

Aristotle (circa 1000 BC) said, "We should conduct ourselves toward others as we would have them act toward us." Buddha echoed this basic concept when he said, "Hurt not others in ways that you yourself would find hurtful." Confucius was even more adamant: "Do unto another what you would have him do unto you, and do not do unto another what you would not have him do unto you." But he also continued, "Thou needest this law alone. It is the foundation of all the rest."

And that same strong sentiment is contained as an essential tenet of major religions. Judaism: "What is hateful to you, do not do to others. This is the entire Law; all the rest is commentary." Hinduism: "Do not do to others what ye do not wish done to yourself…This is the whole Dharma, heed it well."

And the list goes on, but you get the basic idea. Virtually every religion and philosophy espouses this sentiment as a basic tenet of a successful life. Leadership is, obviously, one aspect of life and, therefore, is as bound by this principle as is any other aspect of life. I call it the "Golden Rule of Leadership" (GRL).

The concept is straightforward and simple. But its application is not. The issue is interpretation, or, more accurately, misinterpretation. Remember, the principle is "Treat other people the way you would like to be treated." It is not, "Treat other people the way they treat you."

Yet this latter construction is the way in which many people interpret the principle and that, in turn, dictates the manner of their behavior. It's an understandable misinterpretation. If someone does you harm, "stabs you in the back" (in a figurative, organizational sense), it's difficult not to at least want to reciprocate—to treat them the way they treated you.

And yet that is ultimately a self-destructive response. It can lead to a vicious cycle of reciprocal retaliation. It can create a mindset of "get them before they get you." It fosters a generally applied lack of trust, which inhibits openness, which inhibits credibility, which inhibits building relationships, and on, and on, and on.

The principle is "Treat others the way you would like to be treated." It's a positive, pro-active sentiment. By definition it fosters openness, builds credibility, and enhances the building of relationships—and it helps avoid the negative feelings that foster destructive relationships.

There's also an issue with regard to the definition of leadership itself. Again, there are probably as many definitions of leadership as there are books. But generally, they fall into three major categories: directional leadership, performance leadership, and personal leadership.

Directional leadership, by definition, implies there are other people involved—followers, who are taking the direction of the leader.

Performance leadership—more commonly referred to as "leadership by example"—suggests the leader is not directly leading other people, but rather these other people are observing the leader's behavior, style, attitudes, characteristics, and so on, and attempting to emulate that example.

And personal leadership is just what the name implies—taking responsibility for improving oneself in some way. Other people may not even be aware of the personal leadership an individual is exerting.

In this book we're going to focus on directional leadership, which, again, suggests that there are other people—followers—involved. Someone is leading some others somewhere.

And that takes us to the other key point about directional leadership. It implies change. A leader isn't simply maintaining the status quo, that's the job of the manager, to keep the current business running and viable. To see that the bills are paid. The orders processed. The products shipped. And so on.

The leader is making change—of one sort or another—happen. A change in products, processes or markets. A change in attitude or spirit. A change in customer service.

In fact, if you were to try to summarize leadership as succinctly as possible, you would probably be pretty close to the truth if you simply said, "Leadership is about people and change." The Golden Rule is the compass, the guiding light, for how leaders should deal with the "people" side of leadership. As we mentioned earlier, the essence of leadership is not a process, is not formulaic—leadership is highly individual.

The "change" side of leadership, however, is a process. It is formulaic. "Change" can be represented by frameworks and methodologies. The challenge many leaders have (and that causes many of the failures of leadership we see every day), is that leaders oftentimes mistake the process side of leadership—the "change" portion of it—as the totality of leadership. In fact, as important as it is, change is merely one of the two key elements of leadership, and, of the two, it is by far the lesser in importance.

But even the best-intentioned of leaders who scrupulously follow the Golden Rule, won't succeed without an understanding of, and adherence to, the process side of leadership. So our challenge in this book is to provide the linkage. How does the Golden Rule of Leadership (the "people" side of the leadership equation) apply at every step in the "process" (or "change" side of leadership), and how and why is it essential to the successful execution of each step?

The rest of this book will focus on just that. Each chapter will take—in order—one of the following steps of the process and explain how the application of the Golden Rule facilitates success. While these steps are listed sequentially, they don't necessarily occur in a neat and orderly fashion. There are overlaps. There are steps that occur simultaneously. And it is oftentimes a recursive process. Leaders may have to go back and review or repeat steps to ensure that they are ultimately successfully executed.

One final point about the process. There is no attempt in this book to limit the definition of leadership to senior management levels in an organization. In fact, quite the opposite. Every organization needs leaders at every level in the organization.

But in terms of the process itself, we have assumed that the leadership—or change—effort involves multiple organizational units, including units outside the direct control of the leader. This, I believe, is a more complete and helpful perspective. It's easier to downscale the messages to a smaller or more contained change effort than it would be to upscale to a larger more extensive one. The fundamental process remains the same.

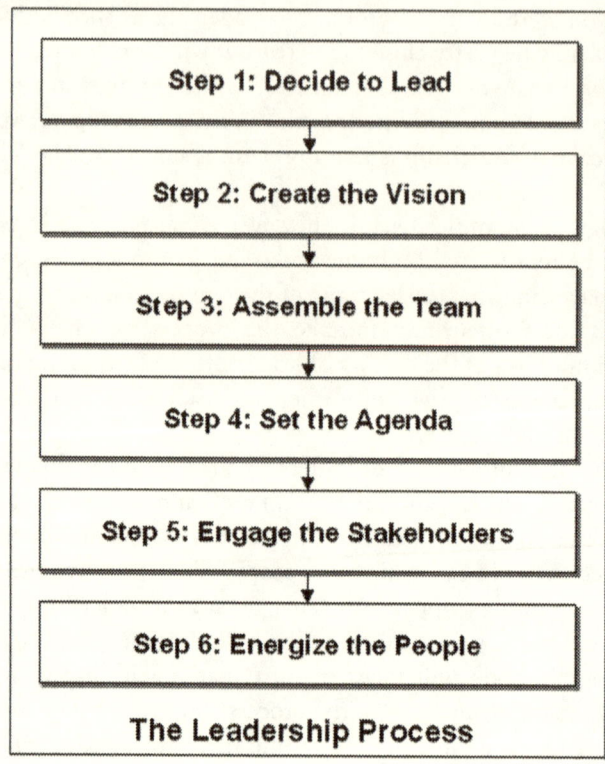

The Leadership Process

The Leadership Process

Step 1: Decide to Lead
Leadership isn't something that simply "happens" to some people and not to others. It's a proactive choice; a conscious decision. And until that decision is made, the rest of the process is merely an academic exercise.

Step 2: Create the Vision
I really didn't want to use the "vision" word (it's so overworked), but I think it captures the thought better than any other (at least any that I could think of). Essentially what it says is, if a leader expects others to follow him or her somewhere, those followers have to know where that "somewhere" is. They have to know where they're going, where they're being led. That's the vision.

Step 3: Assemble the Team

As effective as a leader is, he or she is not going to be successful on his or her own. The era of "rugged individualism" has long since passed. Every leader needs a core team of loyal supporters who will provide assistance and "leadership" during the change process.

Step 4: Set the Agenda

Obviously, having a loyal team wandering aimlessly around trying to help is not going to facilitate success. Team members have to know what their roles are in the change process, what their overarching responsibilities are, and what they need to focus on. That's the purpose of the agenda.

Step 5: Engage the Stakeholders

The definition of the "organization" is dependent on the extent of the leader's responsibilities, the scope of the change effort, and so on. But however that organization is defined, the change effort, ultimately, will not be successful unless it is endorsed and supported—or, at a minimum, accepted—by the business units who may be impacted by that change whether they be inside or outside the direct control of the leader.

Step 6: Energize the People

To succeed in any endeavor that involves changing what people do or how they do it, the leader must ultimately gain the active support and involvement of the people whose roles and/or jobs are being changed. So a major role of the leader is to engage the workforce in the change effort.

A pretty straightforward process. And yet, as we all know, enormously difficult to execute effectively. While accurate statistics are hard to come by, anecdotal evidence suggests that the vast majority of major change efforts either fail completely or only partially succeed.

Why is that? My experience suggests the basic cause of most failures is that while leaders explicitly recognize the importance of "people" (in Step 6), they tend to overlook the "people" part of the equation in the other steps. And yet people are equally, if not more important during those early phases. And that's where the Golden Rule comes in.

In the remainder of this book we'll look specifically at how the Golden Rule can be invoked at every step in the process and why it's so important.

Part I: The Golden Rule of Leadership—Key Points Summary

A. Leadership isn't formulaic. It's not a methodology. Not a process. It's highly individual and there are as many styles of leadership as there are leaders.

B. The Golden Rule of Leadership (GRL). The essence of effective leadership can be summed up in one simple, yet profound statement, "Treat other people the way you would like to be treated." This simple approach fosters openness, builds credibility and enhances the building of relationships.

C. Leadership is about people and change. The GRL is the compass for how leaders should deal with the "people" side of leadership. The "change" side of leadership is a process, which, like all processes, can be represented by frameworks and methodologies.

D. The core message of the GRL is to provide the linkage between the "people" side of leadership and the "change" side of leadership. How does the GRL (the "people" side of the leadership equation) apply at every step in the process of leadership (the "change" side of the leadership equation)? And how and why is the "people" side essential to the successful execution of each step in the leadership process?

E. There are six steps in the Leadership Process

　　1. Decide to Lead. Leadership is a proactive choice.

　　2. Create the Vision. People have to know where they're going—that is, being led—and why.

　　3. Assemble the Team. Every leader needs a core team of loyal supporters who will provide assistance and leadership during the change process.

　　4. Set the Agenda. Team members have to know what their roles and responsibilities are in the change process.

　　5. Engage the Stakeholders. To achieve success, the change effort must be endorsed and supported—or at least accepted—by units outside the direct control of the leader.

　　6. Energize the People. Success depends on gaining the active support and involvement of the people whose roles and/or jobs are being changed.

Pathway to Success
The Golden Rule and the
Leadership Process

Step 1: Decide to Lead

...the most difficult part of any endeavor is taking the first step,
making the first decision.

Robyn Davidson

Rick Pitino has had a storied career in big-time college and professional basketball. He began his "major" career as coach of the Boston University Bulldogs. After a brief stint as an assistant coach for the New York Knicks, he was recruited away by sleepy little Providence College in Rhode Island.

Providence was a good New England basketball school, but not really even considered a regional powerhouse, let alone a national force. Everybody was amazed that a coach of Pitino's stature would go to a school like Providence. It seemed almost like a self-imposed exile from big-time basketball.

His second year there, Pitino took Providence to the final four of the NCAA Tournament. An amazing and unprecedented accomplishment.

From there Pitino was recruited back by the New York Knicks of the NBA, this time as head coach. The Knicks had finished dead last in the NBA the year before and prospects for the coming year appeared dim.

Pitino led them to the playoffs his very first year there. Again, an unheard of accomplishment.

Next stop, the University of Kentucky where Pitino became head coach. In his eight years there, Pitino turned in an unbelievable performance. Five trips to the quarter-finals in the NCAA championships. Three final four appearances. And the biggest prize of all—a national championship. An impressive accomplishment, but by now something that was not surprising for Pitino. His record of success was, if not unparalleled, certainly among the best in the annals of big-time college and professional basketball.

After his success at Kentucky, Pitino was recruited away by the Boston Celtics where he signed a reported ten year, fifty million dollar contract. And it was at this point in time he published a book called *Success is a Choice*. It became an instant business bestseller, and, even though it was widely pooh-poohed by the academic intelligentsia, it was an excellent book, laced throughout with powerful messages.[1]

The basic thesis of the book is that success is not just something that happens to some people and not to others. Success is an active choice people make. And, having made that choice, there are certain things people can do to better prepare themselves to translate that choice into action.

Like success, leadership is also not something that just happens to some people and not to others. It's an active choice people make. And, like success, there are certain things people can do to better prepare themselves to lead.

Leadership is a Choice

The first, and perhaps most important thing people can do is recognize that leadership is, in fact, a choice, and not just a happenstance. Every day, each of us is presented with numerous opportunities to lead. For the most part, for very good and legitimate reasons, most of us let most of these opportunities slip by. Why? We're all too busy to jump at every opportunity that comes our way.

No, we're not suggesting you should leap at every opportunity to lead, but merely that you should take note of all those opportunities, whether you choose to accept the leadership challenge or not. It's only by recognizing those opportunities that you let slip by that you'll be more alert to those opportunities that you really should embrace.

So what sorts of opportunities might come your way? Typically, they fall into three categories.

1. First, are opportunities specifically offered to you—a new project, a promotion, a lateral move to round out your experience base and better prepare you for increased responsibilities, and so on.

2. Second, are opportunities individuals seek out themselves. This list is similar to the one above. It's seeking out new projects, promotions, lateral moves, and so on, all with an aim toward enhancing one's position.

3. And finally, there are what I call situational opportunities for leadership. They are as numerous as the number of people and situations that exist in organizational life, and, therefore, difficult to succinctly summarize. But a few illustrations might resonate with most people.

For example, the weekly conference call that seems to repeat itself every seven days with seemingly nothing ever being accomplished. The meeting that just drones on without any apparent agenda, and again, seemingly without any end in sight. The customer complaint, the stonewalling colleague, the recalcitrant vendor. Opportunities to lead are everywhere.

How do you actually translate the decision to lead into action?

But what does that really mean? How do you actually translate the decision to lead into action in one of these situations?

Let's use the example of the weekly conference call that seems to accomplish nothing, a common frustration among executives and managers with whom I work. Here's the hypothetical situation: A vice-president of operations chairs the call, and participants include a wide hierarchical bandwidth from frontline supervisors to second and third line managers to directors. The purpose is to identify problems, determine required corrective measures, and assign responsibility for taking action.

And each week, that's exactly what happens. And yet, after a few weeks you, a second-level manager—several levels below the vice-president in the hierarchy—realize that the calls tend to be repetitive. The problems are the same each week. The suggested resolutions are the same. The same people are being assigned responsibility for the same types of problems in their areas. It's almost as if one call could have been recorded and replayed every week.

Worse, there never seems to be any attempt to determine whether or not any of the corrective measures were actually implemented, and, if so, whether or not they were successful. The whole thing seems to you to be a fruitless exercise and a complete waste of time.

So what should you do?

Well, if you're like most people, you may decide to do nothing. After all, you're not only not the chairperson of the call, you're not even one of the higher-ranking participants. Why stick your neck out—you might get your head chopped off.

Now, you might think I'm going to criticize that kind of thinking and encourage you to "be a leader," "take charge," or some other such admonishment. Actually, I'm not. Every individual is different and every situation is different. In this case, for any given individual, the decision to do nothing may be entirely appropriate. The important thing isn't whether you do nothing or you do something, the important thing is to recognize that doing nothing or doing something is an active choice—it isn't just something that happens.

Leadership Options are not Binary

That's the first step in becoming a leader—the recognition of leadership opportunities. Most people faced with that situation would do nothing, simply because it wouldn't occur to them to do anything else. A leader recognizes that he or she has options. And, importantly, a leader realizes those options are not binary.

In this case for example, it isn't a matter of, on the one hand, doing nothing, or on the other, attempting to wrest leadership of the meeting from the vice-president—an obviously futile and potentially catastrophic course of action. There's a continuum of potential courses of action—the two listed above are simply the boundaries of that continuum.

So, what else could you do? There are two possible approaches—active and passive. "Active" efforts tend to take the form of statements, suggestions or assertions. They could include things like suggesting the agenda include a review of the last call's "to-do's" to see if there's anything the group could learn from those experiences; or maybe even simply proactively reviewing the results of your own efforts since the last call to set an example for others.

It could mean pointing out that we (i.e., the group) seem to be encountering the same types of problems week after week, and suggesting that maybe there's a way to determine a root cause and develop a systemic solution that would "take care of" a number of these problems and prevent them from recurring. Or it could even be as draconian as asserting that the calls don't seem to be working and suggesting some other approach—perhaps a task force or something along those lines.

"Passive" efforts tend to be more in the nature of questions, probably introduced by some statement of concern or point of order. For example, a request to revisit the objectives of the conference call with an eye toward having the group realize—without your having to explicitly state it—that those objectives are not currently being met, or perhaps don't even exist. Or an expression of concern that we (again, the group) don't seem to be benefiting from each other's experiences and lessons learned, and asking if there's some way those could be included as part of the agenda.

As I'm sure you realize, the point is not the specific nature of the leadership intervention you decide on—or even if you decide to take action. The point is to recognize two things: first, you have a choice, and second, that choice is not binary.

One issue that constantly arises when I have this type of discussion with groups of executives and managers is concern over the reaction of the chairperson—the ranking individual—to whatever course of action you take. What will he or she think? Will he or she be angry, feel threatened, publicly chastise or humiliate you? Or perhaps even take some "behind the scenes" career-inhibiting action.

Unfortunately, there really is no answer to that question. Every situation is unique and different. And the individuals involved are unique and different. And, of course, the actions you take need to comprehend the possibility of those types of repercussions. (Based upon your level of concern, you can scale back your intervention strategy, but potentially still "decide to lead" by taking a more passive approach. If you're not overly concerned—or not concerned at all—you may choose to be a bit more assertive.)

But my general sense is that those worries, while legitimate, are probably, in most instances, misplaced—or at least somewhat exaggerated. More likely the chairperson is just as frustrated as the rest of the group and is looking for someone to step forward with a suggestion that will help break the logjam and help resolve the recurring operational problems.

This example may be small—some may say even trivial. But I would disagree. This is one of the most common complaints of executives and managers—at all levels—with whom I interact. And it serves to illustrate the importance of that initial decision to lead. From my perspective, the very fact that conference calls like the one described in our hypothetical example exist, is de facto evidence of a failure of leadership.

Not an earth-shattering failure, to be sure. But one that hints of the potential for failures in more important matters. At a minimum, it points out the need to be alert to opportunities to exercise leadership, for it's only then that you'll recognize the larger, more important opportunities—the ones that really require a new vision, a coalition of key people to "pull off" the change, a high-level agenda, and so on. For example, the processes that need reengineering. The organizations that need restructuring. The product lines that need new features, functions or designs. The customer service philosophy that needs re-energizing.

"Deciding to Lead" and the Golden Rule

So how does the Golden Rule come into play in this step? To illustrate, let's return to our example. Picture yourself sitting at your desk, your phone tucked against your ear, your fingers tapping impatiently on a pad of white-lined paper.

Knowing that this call is probably going to turn out like all the others. Knowing that there will be no follow-up on previous action items. Knowing that no systemic solution will emerge from the discussion. What would you be hoping would happen on the call? How would you like to be treated?

Well, in our little hypothetical example, you'd probably be delighted if someone on the call took one of the passive or active steps outlined above. Mildly suggesting some of the things you think ought to happen—or perhaps even calling the group to task.

So, if that's the way you'd like to be treated, why not treat other people that way. More than likely many—if not most—of the other participants (perhaps even including the Chair) are thinking the same types of things you are. Wishing that someone—anyone—would step forward and help pull the group out of the quagmire that the conference call had become.

Why not you? Why wait for someone else to "ride to the rescue"—to utter the very words you've been thinking? Emerson said it much better, much more poetically, much more profoundly than I ever could:

> To believe your own thought, to believe that what is true for you in your private heart is true for all men—that is genius. A man should learn to detect and watch that gleam of light which flashes across his mind from within, more than the lustre of the firmament of bards and sages. Yet he dismisses without notice his thought, because it is his. In every work of genius we recognize our own rejected thoughts: they come back to us with a certain alienated majesty. Great works of art have no more affecting lesson for us than this. They teach us to abide by our spontaneous impression with good-humored inflexibility then most when the whole cry of voices is on the other side. Else, tomorrow a stranger will say with masterly good sense precisely what we have thought and felt all the time, and we shall be forced to take with shame our own opinion from another.

"…We shall be forced to take…our own opinion from another." Pretty powerful stuff. We've probably all been there at one time or another. And Emerson's admonition, I believe, can be just as appropriately applied to leadership. We don't want to place ourselves in a position where we must follow our own leadership from another.

Treat people the way you would like to be treated. If you believe that in a given situation some leadership is required, then more than likely other people believe it as well. At a minimum, be alert to that opportunity. And, to be sure, if you decide to exercise leadership, do so intelligently within the context of the situation. Don't wait to be led to the very destination of your own choosing.

To punctuate the point about this first step in the leadership process—"Decide to Lead." It is absolutely essential. Without making the decision to lead, all of the other steps in the process become moot. If you haven't chosen to lead, why develop a vision, why assemble a team and so on? And if you haven't attuned yourself to be alert to those opportunities, don't assume you'll somehow naturally recognize the key ones when they come your way.

Step 1: Decide to Lead—Key Points Summary

A. Leadership is an active choice people make, and there are certain things people can do to better prepare themselves to lead.

B. The first step in becoming a leader is to recognize leadership opportunities. A leader recognizes he or she has options and those options are not binary.

C. Leadership opportunities can be offered to you or sought out by you, or they can be the result of an existing situation.

D. Leadership actions can be "active" or "passive." Active leadership efforts tend to take the form of statements, suggestions, or assertions. Passive leadership efforts tend to be more in the nature of questions, probably introduced by some statement of concern or point of order.

E. The decision to lead is critical. Without that, all of the other steps in the leadership process become moot.

F. When making the decision to lead, remember to apply the GRL.

Pathway to Success
The Golden Rule and the
Leadership Process

Step 2: Create the Vision

The very essence of leadership is that you have to have a vision.

Theodore Hesburgh

The thinking on the importance of having a vision ebbs and flows as the current theories on management and leadership shift, based primarily, I sometimes think, on what the latest bestseller is. But whether it's called vision or something else, it's crucial to any change effort that hopes to be successful.

The reason is simple. If you expect people to follow you, they have to know where you're taking them. It's rare that they'll enthusiastically embark on the journey based on blind faith alone.

Vision Example #1. JFK: "…landing a man on the Moon…"

So, before we begin to discuss how the Golden Rule applies to vision, let's make sure we're on the same page about what a vision is. The best way to do that, I believe, is by example. Perhaps the most widely-referenced example is John F. Kennedy's vision of "…landing a man on the Moon and returning him safely to the Earth."

What makes that articulation of a vision so effective?

First, it's memorable. When that topic comes up, you don't see people rolling their eyes back and struggling to recite by rote some memorized statement. Virtually everybody who is even remotely aware that there was such a vision can replay it almost word for word. And it was more than forty years ago (May 25, 1961) that Kennedy uttered that famous statement!

Second, the vision is clear, concise, and unambiguous. There is no doubt about what Kennedy was determined to do. The vision wasn't couched in a lot of confusing language—it was simple and straightforward. Everyone understood the direction.

Third, it was personal. It captured the imagination of the American people, Kennedy's "followers," if you will. He was taking us to a place we wanted to go. It was exciting, we wanted to be a part of it, even if we were only on the sidelines cheering while others actually sat in the capsule—much like college students share in the thrill of their football team's victories. It was personal. Putting a man on the moon was *our* vision too, not just Kennedy's. And, when we succeeded, it would be *our* victory, not just the victory of whatever administration happened to be "in" at the time.

Fourth, it was motivational. At the time, space was the yardstick by which we measured how we "stacked up" against our primary rival, the Soviet Union. It's perhaps a little difficult today to remember the emotional commitment that we, as a nation, had to the "space race," but we're a competitive people. Most Americans had become concerned that Russia (as the Soviet Union was typically referred to back then) had gained the upper hand. They had bigger rockets, they sent men into space before we did, they put men into orbit before we did, and they were working on a space station before we were. If we were able to put a man on the moon first, that would enable us to retake the lead—and perhaps even breathe a little sigh of relief.

Fifth, it was positive and purposeful, even uplifting. It wasn't couched in negative terminology. It wasn't phrased in desperate terms ("If we don't do this, Russia's going to…"). Kennedy's vision gave America a sense of purpose, a mission, an aspiration to greatness. It motivated us to harness our best energies, our best talents, and drive toward the accomplishment of a goal that had the potential not only to benefit America, but, indeed, the entire world.

Sixth, it was unifying. It gave everyone in America a common goal, a common direction, a common target, a common purpose. You didn't hear anyone challenging the vision, suggesting for example, an alternative target. Or even suggesting that this wasn't an admirable, noble goal. (Granted, you may have heard some voices questioning whether it was the right expenditure of funds at the right time given all the other challenges—poverty, hunger, etc.,—facing the nation. But even these voices weren't critical of the vision, but rather of the priority.)

Seventh, it was inclusive. The American people were involved in the formulation of the vision. Maybe not in any traditional sense—we certainly weren't "polled." People didn't submit suggestions. Interviews and focus groups weren't held, and so on. But we had certainly been conditioned over a period of years to understand the strategic importance of space. Putting a man on the moon had, for centuries, been recognized as kind of an ultimate human achievement. What Kennedy did was tap into the inherent competitive spirit of the American people, harness it, and apply it to the strategic imperative of securing a dominant position in space. The vision was the coalescing instrument that pulled all those things together, and in that sense, the American people were involved in its formulation.

Eighth—and last—it was not encumbered with details. This may seem a little odd as an element of an effective vision, but there was nothing in the vision that gave any hint as to how we (i.e., America) were going to accomplish this incredibly difficult feat. That was going to be left to the rest of us to figure out. Kennedy was merely articulating what the final destination, the final goal, was. He wasn't trying to figure out all the details of how we were going to get there.

So to summarize, what made Kennedy's vision so effective was that it was (1) memorable, (2) clear, concise, and unambiguous, (3) personal, (4) motivational, (5) positive, (6) unifying, (7) inclusive, and (8) not encumbered with details. That pretty much sums up what it takes to develop an effective vision.

Vision Example #2. Pike Place Fish, Seattle: "Be World Famous"[2]

Let's look at another example, Pike Place Fish in Seattle. For years a sleepy little fish store in Seattle's quaint public market area. A new owner, Johnny Yokoyama (then a mere twenty-five-year-old) bought the store from the previous owner in 1965 primarily because he believed it would be easier to make the payments on his new Buick Riviera on an owner's salary than on an employee's wage. For a time, Johnny ran the market pretty much the same as it had always been run. Then one of the employees—a young person, as Johnny would say—suggested they ought to try and become "world famous."

Johnny's initial reaction was to chuckle at what he thought was a kind of ridiculous notion. After all, he reasoned, how could a rather unremarkable fish market become world famous?

And then, the more he thought about it, the more he "got into" the idea. Why not? Why couldn't they do it?

He gathered his team together (basically all the employees) and they talked about it and decided to go for it. Their official vision: Be World Famous. The words of the initial suggestion. No attempt to reconstruct it into some lofty sounding phrase. No attempt to complicate it by trying to figure out how they were going to become world famous. All that would be left to the journey itself. All they knew was the final destination.

Does this qualify as an effective vision? Let's examine the elements. First, is it memorable? Certainly. I doubt very much that there are any employees at Pike Place Fish that couldn't easily articulate what the vision is.

Second, is it clear, concise, and unambiguous? Again, yes. In fact, so simple and straightforward as to almost sound naïve. And, in fact, Johnny might actually agree that's exactly what it was—naïve.

Third, was it personal? Was it something everyone at Pike Place Fish could relate to, could "get into"? This, of course, is a question for the employees of Pike Place Fish. But the answer, I think, is clearly "yes." Think of it this way. Would you like to be a clerk in a fish store doing what is certainly honorable and necessary work, but which is, nonetheless a job that is cold and physically demanding? Or would you prefer to be world famous? The employees were excited about the vision. It was an opportunity to do something—to *be* something—that they had never before dreamed.

Fourth, was it motivational? The response here is probably a repeat of the above comments. The opportunity to become world famous clearly motivated the employees to think differently about themselves and their jobs. To approach what they did and how they did it with a different attitude. To deal differently with the customers.

Fifth, was it positive? The answer is clearly yes. Granted, it's possible to become world famous by doing negative things. But it was, and is, intuitively obvious that the attempt was to become world famous by doing "good" things.

Sixth, was it unifying? The answer, again, I believe, is clearly "yes." I suspect some employees (probably now long since gone) weren't interested. Some may have simply wanted to work their hours and take home their paychecks (and there's nothing necessarily wrong with that). But, for the most part, people rallied around the vision. It created a shared sense of excitement. It was, I suspect, a major topic of conversation during coffee breaks and lunch hours.

Seventh, were the people involved in the development of the vision? Clearly, "yes." In fact, it was really the "people" (in the form of one young employee) who actually proposed the "vision," although it probably was not couched in "vision" terms. And Johnny didn't let it rest there. He held group meetings, got "buy-in" to the vision, charged everyone with the responsibility to personalize it, to determine—for themselves—how they could make a contribution to its ultimate achievement. In fact, Johnny went so far as to coach the members of the entire team that they (i.e., each individual employee) would actually lose power if all they did was "accept" the vision. The more they personalized it, the more they would "own" it, and the more power they would have to make it happen.

And, finally, was it unencumbered with details? Again, obviously "yes." In fact, Johnny admits he didn't have any idea as to how they were going to achieve this vision. But, in retrospect, he has commented that it was amazing how, once they had committed to the vision, the things they had to do to get there became clearer.

There's the checklist. Was the Pike Place Fish vision of being world famous effective? According to our checklist, the answer is a resounding "yes."

But how about the results? Did it actually become world famous? Well, fortunately for us (from a learning perspective), and for them (from a business perspective) the results are in. Pike Place Fish is now one of the premier attractions in Seattle. It's been featured on television specials. It's been used as a backdrop for commercials for other companies and products. Camera crews from literally around the world have come to film the remarkable "happening" that Pike Place Fish has become.

So what did they do? How did they accomplish this remarkable feat? Interestingly, in essence what they did is apply the Golden Rule. They focused on the customer and, in everything they did, they implicitly asked, "If I were the customer, how would I like to be treated?"

Well, they decided they'd like to have fun rather than simply plod through a dreary old fish market. So instead of carrying customer purchases to the cash register, they threw them. Instead of mechanically answering customers' questions, they engaged in some good-natured bantering with them. Instead of just performing their duties, they performed. Dancing, joking, kidding around with the customers—a real, live, working "Fish Market Improv!"

Vision and the Golden Rule

How about your vision—or, perhaps more to the point—your organizational unit's vision. How does it stack up against this checklist?

1. [ ] Is it memorable?

2. [ ] Is it clear, concise, and unambiguous?

3. [ ] Is it personal?

4. [ ] Is it motivational?

5. [ ] Is it positive?

6. [ ] Is it unifying?

7.   [ ] Is it inclusive?

8.   [ ] Is it unencumbered with details?

More than likely in many cases the immediate, honest answer would be, "We don't have a vision." And so the real question is, how do you develop one? What's the process?

That takes us back to the Golden Rule. Treat other people the way you would like to be treated. Would you prefer to be "handed" a vision and told this is where we (i.e., the organizational unit) are going to go, or would you rather be invited to participate in the determination of the vision? The answer, I think, is clearly the latter.

So, if you're in a position that requires you to develop a vision, remember how you would like to be treated and treat the people in your organization that way. Don't "impose" a vision on them; find some way to involve them in a process that results in the vision.

Vision "Drivers"

That's rarely easy to do, but I maintain it is always possible. Three potential forces compel an organization to develop a vision, in no particular order.

The first is management initiative. Senior management simply believes (as I do) that it is important for people in the organization to have a sense of direction, to understand where the organization is headed. Jack Welch essentially did this when he took over the reins at General Electric (GE) in the early eighties and established a vision that every business unit in GE would be number one or two in its industry.

The second is legislative or regulatory mandate. Something occurs which fundamentally changes the ground rules in the industry and requires organizations to rethink their direction and mission. This is precisely the situation that occurred in the telecommunications industry in the mid- to late-nineties with the passage of the Telecommunications Act of 1996. Monopolistic control over geographic territories was going away; traditional "phone companies" were forced to rethink their entire businesses.

And the third is environmental (particularly competitive) impetus. For example, a new competitor emerges which fundamentally changes either the economics or the nature of competition in an industry. Toyota did both of these things in the automobile industry when it consistently, year after year, improved quality and, at the same time, reduced both their own internal cost structure and, often, the price to the end customer.

Do You Need a Vision?

So, the first question in the "vision process" is, do you need a vision? Assuming you are not in a situation where your vision is being driven by government mandate or competitive pressures, should management initiate a vision effort?

To answer that, let's go back to the elements of a vision and see whether they are intrinsically worthwhile.

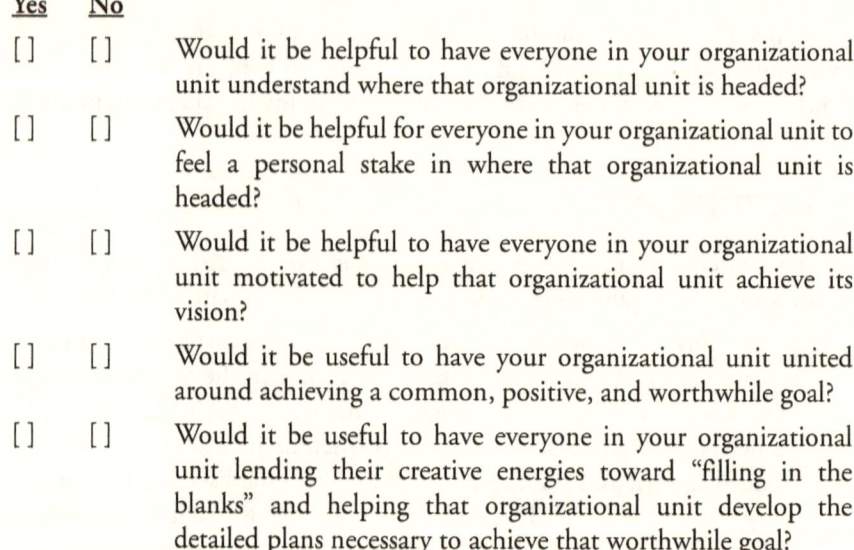

Yes	No	
[ ]	[ ]	Would it be helpful to have everyone in your organizational unit understand where that organizational unit is headed?
[ ]	[ ]	Would it be helpful for everyone in your organizational unit to feel a personal stake in where that organizational unit is headed?
[ ]	[ ]	Would it be helpful to have everyone in your organizational unit motivated to help that organizational unit achieve its vision?
[ ]	[ ]	Would it be useful to have your organizational unit united around achieving a common, positive, and worthwhile goal?
[ ]	[ ]	Would it be useful to have everyone in your organizational unit lending their creative energies toward "filling in the blanks" and helping that organizational unit develop the detailed plans necessary to achieve that worthwhile goal?

Let's assume you've answered "yes" to these questions. You've decided it makes sense for your organizational unit to develop a vision. The question then becomes, how do you go about doing it? Since the key thesis of this book is the importance of the Golden Rule—treating people the way you would like to be treated—and since we've already discussed how you, if you were in such a situation, would like to be included in the "vision process," we'll review only those methods of developing a vision that involve the people.

That is not to suggest, of course, that there are no other methods—and certainly not to suggest there are no approaches to developing a vision that do not include involving the people. Clearly there are. In fact, it would be my guess that most "visions" have been developed without the involvement of those people who would be most affected by that vision. Jack Welch's "Number 1 or Number 2" vision, I suspect, was not the result of some comprehensive inclusive process, but may have been much closer to a kind of "vision by fiat."

And the reality is that there are times when such an approach is called for. If, for example, your company or business unit is faced with a new and significant—and perhaps unexpected—competitive threat, it may require dramatic and immediate action to counter that threat. You may not have time to "engage" all the people in the development of a vision.

But even in a circumstance like that, it's in your best interest to, at a minimum, educate the people about what that competitive threat is and why such dramatic action is called for. They may not "like" the vision, but at least they'll better understand the need for it and hopefully rally around it.

How to Involve People in Developing a Vision

Having noted that, then, here are the four "inclusive" ways to develop a vision, in no particular order of importance.

1. **Direction.** The "leader" determines where the organization (the people) must go, provides information to the organization—educates the people, if you will, regarding the driving forces behind the coming vision—and then announces it to the organization. This is probably what happened when Lou Gerstner took over the reins at IBM. By most accounts, the company was in trouble. Its market share was down. Debt was up. According to some industry experts, the mainframe—IBM's staple for some forty years—was "dead." And IBM was an also-ran in the PC market.

    Even though he is famous for stating, "The last thing IBM needs right now is a vision,"[3] Gerstner announced one: IBM would "…lead big companies into the brave new networked world."[4] He drove the vision into the organization, scrapped plans for breaking IBM up, shook up the culture and refocused IBM on the mainframe and PC businesses while driving relentlessly toward a leadership position in the new networked world.

    A vision born of a consensus-building process? Probably not. But more than likely it captured the spirit of—and re-energized—an organization that had been buffeted by setbacks over the past decade. And the results demonstrate the wisdom and power of that vision. IBM is back. Revenues and profits are up. The stock has recovered. And nobody these days is talking about burying IBM.

2. **Consensus Building.** The "leader" determines where the organization must go and then, through words, deeds, examples, announcements, memos, white papers, management letters, and, often, a formal program of educa-

tion, persuades the organization of the need for—and wisdom of—the vision. Traditional phone companies are good examples here. When it became clear that technological advances were going to render the traditional monopolistic telephone business structure obsolete and that deregulation would provide the necessary legislative support for competitive forays into non-traditional markets and products, a number of RBOC's (Regional Bell Operating Companies) and other independent telephone companies launched comprehensive internal PR and educational efforts to prepare their organizations for the coming radical changes.

3. **Democracy.** The "leader" recognizes the need for a vision, but believes it is ultimately in the organization's best interest if the people have a direct role in the development of that vision. Pike Place Fish is a good example here. Even though "Johnny" had the final "say-so" regarding what the vision was, he involved the entire organization in the process.

4. **Representation.** Analogous to a republic versus a democracy, in a representative process the "leader" involves the entire organization, but not all the employees—at least not directly. Toyota does this as a matter of course. The frontline associates (Toyota calls them "team members") select colleagues to represent them in various company initiatives—training them on new model vehicles, for example. In this example, those representatives then come back and transfer what they've learned to their fellow team members.

The choice of method is dependent partially on the urgency of the situation, partially on the size of the organizational unit, and, importantly, partially on the clarity (at least from the "leader's" perspective) of what the vision must be. Think of it as a two-step decision process. The first step is to determine whether or not the vision has really already been decided on, or whether there is any flexibility.

If the vision is truly a fait accompli, then the worst thing a leader can do is pretend otherwise, bring the organization through some sort of faux involvement process, and then "spring" the predetermined result on them. No. If the vision has already been determined, then the leader must either employ *Direction* or *Consensus Building* to engage the employees in the effort to achieve the vision.

If, on the other hand, the vision has not been predetermined, then both the *Democratic* and *Representative* approaches are also open to the leader. The decision as to which to use is a function of the size of the organizational unit and of the urgency of the situation. Think of it as a kind of decision matrix:

Urgency of Situation	Size of Organization	Pre-Determined Vision	Vision To Be Determined
Not Urgent	Large or Small Organization	Consensus Building	Democracy
Urgent	Large Organization	Directive	Representative
	Small Organization	Consensus Building	Democracy

Basically the decision process breaks down this way: If the vision is predetermined, then the available options are *Directive* or *Consensus Building*. If it's not, then *Representative* or *Democracy* are the potential courses of action.

The trade-offs between *Directive* and *Consensus Building* are speed and strength of buy-in and commitment. A *Directive* approach is typically faster, but *Consensus Building* tends to build more ownership.

The trade-offs between *Representative* and *Democracy* are similar. *Representative* tends to be quicker, but *Democracy* inherently has more personal involvement, and, hence, a potentially stronger buy-in.

If the vision has been predetermined, the next question is, how urgent is the situation that has created the need for the vision? If it isn't particularly urgent, then *Consensus Building* is probably the right approach. You have the time to present your vision, explain the benefits, and build the case. The "people" have the time to digest the information, internalize the benefits, and "buy-into" your logic.

If, however, the situation is urgent, then the size of the organization becomes a factor. If it's a large organization, then *Directive* is probably your only realistic alternative because that can be done much faster than *Consensus Building* in a large organization. If it's a smaller organization, on the other hand, then it may be possible to build consensus nearly as quickly as it would be to take a *Directive* approach.

If the vision has not been predetermined, the next question is still, how urgent is the situation? If it's not particularly urgent, then *Democracy* may be the best approach.

If, however, there is a pressing need, then the next question again is, how large is the organization? For a large organization with a pressing need, *Representative* may be the best approach. For a smaller organization, you may have the time to execute a more democratic process.

Either way, of course, it isn't the process that's important—any one that works will do. It's the end result that counts. Does the vision meet the eight criteria of an effective vision: (1) memorable, (2) clear, (3), personal (4) motivational, (5) positive, (6) unifying, (7) inclusive, and (8) unencumbered with details?

Step 2: Create the Vision—Key Points Summary

A. If you expect people to follow you, they have to know where you're taking them. Whether you call it "vision" or something else, it's crucial to any change effort that hopes to be successful.

B. A vision is effective when: (1) it is memorable; (2) it is clear, concise, and unambiguous; (3) it captures the imagination; (4) it is motivational; (5) it is positive and purposeful; (6) it is unifying; (7) people involved in supporting the vision are somehow involved in the formulation of the vision; and (8) there is nothing in the vision statement that even hints as to how the vision will be accomplished.

C. The GRL of creating the vision: If you're in a position that requires you to develop a vision, find someway to involve the people in your organization in the process that results in the vision.

D. There are four inclusive ways to develop a vision:

1. Direction. The leader determines where the organization (people) must go, announces the vision, and educates the organization.

2. Consensus Building. The leader determines where the organization must go and then, through words, deeds, examples, announcements, memos, white papers, etc., persuades the organization of the need for and wisdom of the vision.

3. Democracy. The leader recognizes the need for a vision, but believes it is ultimately in the organization's best interest if the people have a direct role in the development of the vision.

4. Representation. Analogous to a republic versus a democracy, in a representative process the leader involves the entire organization, but not all the employees, at least not directly.

Pathway to Success
The Golden Rule and the
Leadership Process

Step 3: Assemble the Team

We don't accomplish anything in this world alone...

Sandra Day O'Connor

The era of rugged individualism, if it ever really existed, has long since passed—at least in an organizational sense. It's virtually impossible to get things done in organizations today, regardless of size, without engaging a team of committed individuals who are willing—even enthusiastic about—supporting the vision. Let's call this group your *Cabinet*.

One natural question that arises then is, who should be on this Cabinet? But a second, equally important question is, who should *not* be on it? Remembering that leadership is about change, and that the vision sets the direction for that change, there are going to be people who support the vision (i.e., the "change"), and people who oppose it. The reality of organizational life is that we must deal with both.

There are two common schools of thought on whether to include the "opposers" in your Cabinet. One school says only include those people who are supporters of your efforts. The other says include all key stakeholders, even if they are neutral or opposed.

There are two basic arguments in favor of inclusion. As you might suspect, the first is the Golden Rule. If positions were reversed, and you were potentially going to be impacted by what another group was doing, how would you like to be treated? Wouldn't you want to be included; wouldn't you want to have a voice? Then the logic of the GRL would suggest that you should treat other people the same way. Include them; give them a voice.

The second argument is more pragmatic. Remember the old saying, "It's better to have someone inside your tent throwing stones out, than outside your tent throwing stones in." It gives you an opportunity to influence their thinking. It eliminates any potential complaints they may have about not being included. And, if your efforts at influencing their thinking are unsuccessful, it gives you an opportunity to deal with their objections, prepare an appropriate response, and develop and implement a plan to overcome—or override—them.

The downside to this approach (i.e., the argument against inclusion) is the non-supporters on your team will have complete knowledge of everything you're doing, and, therefore, be in a better position to undermine it, should they so desire. The counter-argument is it gives you an opportunity to build a relationship with them, to hear their objections (some, or many, of which may be perfectly legitimate and logical), and possibly counter their arguments or adjust your approach to mute any perceived negative impacts.

A Two-Tier Structure

Sound arguments on both sides of the fence, so what do you do—include or not include? The answer, I believe, is do both—include *and* not include. How? By implementing a third approach. One that honors the Golden Rule without potentially undermining your efforts to achieve your vision. That is to form, in addition to your Cabinet, a second body. Let's call it the *Stakeholder Committee,* or simply the *Committee.* In brief, the Cabinet consists solely of supporters of the vision; the Committee may include some, or all members of the Cabinet, but also, importantly, other key stakeholders, some of whom may be opposed to the vision.

This approach allows you a forum (the Cabinet) where you can speak openly, plan strategy, discuss options for overcoming objections, neutralizing the opposition, and so on. But, through the Committee, it also allows you to include the opposition, give them a voice, respond to objections, and potentially devise accommodations that respect their legitimate concerns, and so on.

So, the logical question is who, specifically, should be included in each of these groups? And, just as important, what would be expected of them, and how do you ensure each group operates effectively?

Who Should be Included on the Cabinet and the Committee?

This is actually the easy question. As we stated above, the Cabinet should consist solely of your key allies and supporters. Your confidants. People who believe in the vision and are as enthusiastic about achieving it as you are. And, importantly, people who are willing to speak out and express their views openly and honestly about how to go about achieving that vision, even if they're not in complete agreement with views. (It's been said that one of the reasons for the Bay of Pigs fiasco during Kennedy's administration was that no one on his "Cabinet" was willing to dissent. No one wanted to be perceived to be a "naysayer.")

The Committee, on the other hand, should consist of all other key stakeholders, including those who are neutral or opposed to the vision.

Some might say that supportive stakeholders should also be invited to join the Cabinet, but I disagree, for two reasons. First, by being *inclusive*, you are also, by definition, being *exclusive*. That is, since you won't be able to include all stakeholders in your Cabinet, you will clearly be leaving some out. Potential supporters who are "left out" may feel rejected or unwanted, and may, in fact, resent their exclusion—even, potentially, to the point where their support swings the other way.

The second reason is that you don't want the Committee populated solely by "opposers" and "naysayers." You want supporters included in that group to balance the discussion and counterbalance potential arguments against the vision.

"Inclusion on the Committee" and the Golden Rule

So the question then becomes who, specifically, are those stakeholders who should be included on the Committee? At a minimum, you need to involve any organizational unit on whose support the success of your vision depends. So, for example, if you anticipate you'll be redefining jobs, or adding or eliminating positions, or changing the compensation and/or incentive and reward systems, then a representative of human resources should absolutely be a member of the team.

Why? Well, let's go back to the Golden Rule. If you were in the human resources function and somebody else was potentially doing the things discussed above—and ultimately impacting your area of responsibility—wouldn't you want "in" on the process that resulted in these changes?

More pragmatically, since you'll ultimately be looking for "approval" of these changes, you want to be sure they have the "blessing" of the "approvers" before going too far down that road. The best way to do that is get their ownership and "buy-in" by including them during the process.

The finance organization is essentially the same issue. If achieving your vision will involve budget increases, capital investments, etc., then clearly finance will need to be involved.

And possibly—or, perhaps more accurately, likely—so will the information technology organization. If achieving your vision will require new systems, or modifications to existing systems, then I/T must be involved as well.

It may not be possible to fully anticipate everyone who may ultimately need to be involved, but I believe it's possible to make a pretty good stab at it. Other departments—upstream or downstream from your area of responsibility. Other staff functions. Potentially, other stakeholders who may not—at least on the surface—appear to be directly involved. It just takes a few minutes thought and you can come up with a pretty good list. To beat the drum one more time, think of the Golden Rule. What other functions or positions might potentially be impacted (either positively or negatively) by your attempts to achieve your vision? If you were in one of these other functions or positions, wouldn't you want to be included? So, act accordingly.

What is Expected of Team (i.e., Cabinet and Committee) Members

The roles of the Cabinet and Committee are different, and what is expected of members of each group is, accordingly, different.

The Cabinet

The Cabinet basically serves as your personal advisory board. While their exact functions may be as varied as the individuals who work with such groups, there are some general duties that each may be expected to perform:

❖ Enthusiastically support and promote the vision.

❖ Participate in the development of a high-level agenda helping to determine strategies—as appropriate and necessary—for any implications regarding organizational structure, required systems (e.g., information technology, compensation and incentive, etc.), job definitions/responsibilities, skills required, and so on.

❖ Define roles and responsibilities for members of the Cabinet and diligently perform any assigned tasks.

❖ "Sell" the vision to stakeholders.

❖ Motivate employees to enthusiastically support the vision and engage in efforts to achieve it.

There's no magic here. You want team (i.e., Cabinet) members who will be actively involved, who will enthusiastically support the effort to achieve the vision, and who will help provide leadership to the employees and the rest of the organization.

The (Stakeholder) Committee

The Committee is more analogous to a user group in the software industry. There, users (i.e., stakeholders) of a software company's products meet periodically to learn about what's happening in the company (e.g., product enhancements, new products, etc.), air their issues and problems with the software they've purchased, get progress reports on any "fixes" or updates to the software based upon their previous input, and suggest ideas for product enhancements or new products to the company. They do not have the authority to "dictate" to the company, but good software companies take their input seriously, and get back to the users with decisions—either positive or negative—on previous suggestions.

The Committee serves a similar function. It doesn't have the right to "dictate" to the proponents of the vision, but wise proponents will take their input seriously. The Committee has three basic functions:

❖ Learn about your efforts to achieve the vision.

❖ Share issues, concerns, and problems with the vision and your efforts to achieve the vision.

❖ Cooperate with you to resolve those potential obstacles to success. This may include suggesting alternative approaches that may help avoid problems.

No small task, to be sure, but relatively straightforward. For the most part, roles and responsibilities will be fairly clear. The human resources representative (assuming there is one on the team) will be responsible for surfacing—and helping to develop resolutions for—issues related to employees: headcount allocations, benefits implications, and compensation, reward and incentive issues, and so on. The finance team member would have similar responsibilities related to budget and capital allocations. And so on with representatives from other staff functions.

Representatives from line organizations will have philosophically similar, but operationally different roles. For example, team members who have responsibility for processes upstream or downstream from the leader's, will potentially need to develop operational changes in the "handoffs" to and from the leader's process. They will need to build awareness and support throughout their organizations for the coming changes. And they may need to participate in joint planning sessions with the leader and members of his or her organization to map out any potential changes in the operational linkages between the organizational units.

Expectations and the GRL

Again, remember the Golden Rule. If you were a representative from one of these other areas, how would you like to be treated? The people in these other areas have a strong personal vested interest in how they may be impacted by what you're doing. They shouldn't be included on the team simply as a matter of "form," to simply observe or "rubber stamp" what you're doing. Rather, they should have a substantive voice that can potentially impact what you're doing.

But what does that mean from your perspective? It means you must be prepared to make adjustments to your plan and/or timing—perhaps even to your "vision"—in order to accommodate concerns raised by other members of the team. Not to the point that you seriously undercut your own efforts, of course. But more than likely you will need partners, and you want those partners to have a stake in the positive outcome of your endeavor. The only way to create that "stake" is to give them all a sense of ownership, and the only way to do that is to give them a legitimate voice.

How to Ensure the Team Operates Effectively

This is the trickiest one. It's one thing to invite people to join a team and to outline their roles and responsibilities, it's quite another to get them to function effectively together as a team.

In our work with thousands of executives and managers over the past fifteen years, we've found that, almost without exception, they are able to clearly articulate what it takes to make a team effective. Yet, when asked to evaluate the performance of teams that they have personally been on (i.e., not *their* performance on the teams, but rather the overall performance of the team itself), they rank it at an average of about six on a scale of one to ten. And, while there are outliers on both the upside and downside, the overall bandwidth is rather narrow, ranging from about five and a half to about seven.

Clearly the knowledge is not being translated into performance. The question is why? How do we explain this apparent paradox, and what can we do to correct it? We've found that there are a number of reasons why competent, effective executives and managers are not able to translate their knowledge into action. The first is probably the most visibly obvious, and probably the easiest to overcome—the number of people on the team. But there are three other primary causes of less-than-optimal team performance: Teams often fail to establish—upfront—a set of working "ground rules," members are often geographically remote from each other, and teams often fail to execute an effective "team process" that will lead to high performance. Let's take each one in turn.

Number of People

When we've polled executives and managers on the number of people on teams they've been on, the overall range is huge, extending from three or four to over one hundred. But the "Bell Curve Bulge" is rather narrow, the average being around twenty with a bandwidth of about fifteen to twenty-five.

Yet, to a person, these same executives and managers, when asked what they believed the "ideal" team size to be, said ten was the maximum, and their average "optimal" size ranged from six to eight. Our research confirms that most "experts" agree—they suggest team sizes in the range of five to nine.

Of course, executives and managers rightly protest that they rarely have control over team size—rather, they are typically asked (or told) to participate on a team where the size has already been predetermined. So what do you do then? Is that team pre-ordained to fail?

To differentiate between what executives and managers told us about the ideal team size, and what their actual experience tended to be, let's call the smaller group (i.e., ten or fewer members) a *team*, and groups with more than ten members a *committee*.

The challenge "our" executives and managers told us about was that they ended up sitting on what was, in effect, a committee (even though it was called a team), and it was very difficult to get anything done. Too many people. Too many agendas. Not enough focus.

But not everyone had that experience. Those who were successful told us they succeeded because they "subdivided" the committee into smaller groups. Groups that were able to really function as a team. Everyone in the smaller group was bought into its mission. They had specific goals and objectives. Roles and responsibilities. They communicated effectively, both internally and externally.

The central message from all this, I suppose, is that the decision regarding the number of people on the team is important. There's nothing inherently wrong with a committee (as we've defined it), but if you want to perform at higher levels, then you've got to find "work-arounds"—like subdividing—to overcome the inertia that's built into the committee structure.

So how does all this "play into" our two-tier structure of the *Cabinet* and the (Stakeholder) *Committee*? Clearly, the Cabinet is a group who we want to ensure is capable of operating as a high-performance team. In terms of size, that means six to eight people; in most situations I wouldn't think this would be a problem.

You want a relatively small group of loyal supporters "leading the charge." A group who is mainly in concert both with the direction and the approach, whose members trust each other, and can make decisions quickly.

The Committee, on the other hand, (again, in terms of size) is, in effect, just what we've described above. It may very well have more—perhaps many more—than six to eight members. From your perspective as leader of this change effort, it's probably not necessary that it operate as a high-performance team. If and when that level of performance is required, the Committee can probably be sub-divided into smaller groups that can, in fact, operate at that higher level of performance.

Ground Rules

At the beginning of almost every team effort there tends to be an understandable, but naïve, expectation that everybody share the same goals, that everybody will work equally hard, and that the members will work well together and share the credit for any successes. Yet the reality of the team experience rarely meets these rosy expectations.

There are often multiple interpretations of what the team's mission is. Hidden agendas and conflicting objectives often undermine the team's efforts. Some members work hard, others don't. And the reality is that there are often team members who pay lip service to the ideal of "there is no 'I' in team," but who actually seek out individual glory.

That's life. There are some things teams simply aren't going to be able to impact—human nature, for example. But having a set of clear, concise, and mutually agreed upon ground rules will make it much easier for the team to operate effectively and productively, and to deal with situations that can potentially undermine team performance. This is merely an explicit operationalization of the Golden Rule. Put yourself in the other person's shoes. How would you like to be treated? Wouldn't you want to know what's expected of you, and not just from a roles and responsibilities perspective, but also from a "valued team member" perspective? Wouldn't you want some assurance that the team is going to operate in a manner consistent with how you would expect a good team to operate? And so on.

Then treat other people the same way. Ensure there is a set of operating ground rules that team members understand and buy into. The best way to do that, of course, is to allow them to develop—or at least participate in the development of—those ground rules. Your role may be simply to ensure that, at a minimum, those ground rules address poor performance, team dynamics, scope creep, and internal and external communications.

Ground Rule: Poor Performance

Ideally, everyone on the team will give his or her best efforts at all times. Unfortunately that's rarely the case. In our experience, most teams have one or more members who, for a variety of reasons ranging from overwork to lack of interest to insufficient knowledge or skills, just simply don't "pull their own weight." Without a guideline that has been established and agreed to "up front" by all members, it can be very difficult to deal with these situations. But with such a guideline, it becomes a relatively straightforward process—not easy, not comfortable, and certainly not fun—but at least straightforward. Typically, it's then simply a matter of invoking the guideline and taking the agreed upon steps, which may include things like:

1. Alerting the individual that his or her performance is not acceptable, and explaining in detail what is expected of them.

2. Outlining a follow-up plan to monitor anticipated performance improvements.

3. Explaining what action will be taken if performance does not improve.

4. Taking whatever action has been deemed appropriate.

Ground Rule: Team Dynamics

Like any organizational structure—for that matter, any human endeavor—teams cannot escape the infinite variety of personal styles and interpersonal relationships. What is particularly important for a team; however, is to decide how to deal with them in a manner that enables effective team performance. Some simple guidelines can help, particularly related to the following:

❖ **Punctuality.** Some people are almost pathologically punctual; others are just the opposite. In normal business settings, I suppose one might say that whatever works for you is fine. Even in a team setting, chronic lateness might be acceptable if that tends to be the norm.

  If not, however, being chronically late for meetings, conference calls, etc., can cause some real strain. The team simply has to make some decisions about punctuality, make it clear what's expected, and then fall back on this guideline if there are chronic abusers.

  I will say, however, that in my experience, people who are chronically late are chronically late—they seem to operate on a different internal clock than those who tend to be punctual. There simply may not be much you can do about it. So my suggestion is to establish a guideline and call chronic abusers to task, but don't make any "penalties" too draconian. You need to leave yourself some "wiggle room" for those high performers who also happen to be chronically late.

❖ **Participation.** This is an important one. People are different. They have different styles. They have different comfort levels when it comes to speaking in a group setting. But when it comes to team performance it may not be acceptable for someone to simply sit on the sidelines without participating simply because that's their "comfort zone."

I believe in this case it's up to the team—and perhaps especially the team leader—to help bring a normally quiet person into the conversations. Oftentimes they're anxious to participate, they simply don't know how to do it, or they may be too shy or embarrassed to speak up—perhaps for fear of being "wrong" or saying something others may think is irrelevant, maybe even stupid. Of course these fears are rarely justified, but they may be very real to the person experiencing them.

Nominal Group Technique

So how do you bring such a person into the discussions? One way is to employ the "nominal group technique," particularly in early team meetings. That simply says that, instead of just allowing people to jump in and talk whenever they want to contribute something, the team leader (or facilitator, if there is one) will go around the room asking for comments by each person in turn. "Passing" is not acceptable. After a couple of rounds like this, the floor can be opened up for general comments.

Coaching

A second way is simply to coach the individual who is uncomfortable speaking up. The team leader could do this, but it's also very appropriate for another team member who may be closer to the individual to take him or her aside and help them get more comfortable.

Of course, it's not just the quiet members who are potentially of concern. There is also the opposite issue—the team member who seems to try and dominate every discussion. In many ways, this is actually a more challenging situation. You don't want to "kill" the participation, you just want to manage it a bit.

The same two methods apply here. The nominal group technique, which can be used to help draw out quieter members, can also be used to tone down the more talkative members. And coaching can also be an effective tool.

Dealing with the Iconoclast

Perhaps the most difficult situation is the one in which there is someone who views him or herself as the resident "devil's advocate," the iconoclast, the "group conscience." While it's sometimes helpful for this role to be played in the group, it can also be a destructive influence. Less assertive or forceful members can sometimes be intimidated by a more aggressive teammate. This can stifle discussion, inhibit creative interchanges, and lead to a "one-person" plan.

Oftentimes one understandable human reaction to this type of behavior is to "clam up." (After all, who among us wants to subject him or herself to ridicule or sarcastic and cutting remarks?)

The other common reaction is to "respond in kind." To "take on" the aggressor. But this can be disastrous. More than likely he or she is more prac-ticed—and better—at it than you are. They may even relish the challenge of "beating" you at their game.

So how do you deal with this situation? Let's turn to the Golden Rule. How would you like to be treated? Well, most of us would like to be treated with respect. We'd like our opinions and comments to be heard, taken seri-ously and, if the group agrees with them, adopted. So let's apply that think-ing to the "aggressor" in our little example. Instead of assuming the remarks are intended to be "wise," assume they're intended to be taken seriously, and respond that way. Treat them with respect. Rephrase them, dropping the potentially sarcastic and/or offensive tone. Choose to lead. Suggest the group consider the newly-phrased comment carefully. Discuss it. If it, in fact, does make sense, move forward with it. If not, explain why and move past it.

Treating the remark as a serious suggestion will tend to put the aggressor in a bit of an awkward situation. They either have to "own up" to the fact that it wasn't meant to be taken seriously, which may subject them to some implicit criticism for wasting the team's time. Or they have to just "let it go," in which case their credibility may suffer a bit of a black eye. In either case, they may be more reluctant to try the "wise-crack" technique the next time around.

Hopefully that approach will work. If it doesn't, you're left with three alternatives. As we noted above, one is the nominal group technique. Unfortunately this is oftentimes not as effective as it is in the other situations simply because the aggressive member can sometimes refuse to "play by the rules," or make side comments that are purportedly intended to be humor-ous, but which are actually oftentimes cutting and sarcastic. And, while it's possible coaching can help, that's only if the "iconoclast" is amenable to being coached.

No, the unfortunate reality is that sometimes the only way to deal with this situation is by firmly invoking whatever appropriate guideline has been established—full participation, respect for each other's opinions, non-judgmental, and so on, and by taking whatever action has been agreed upon in advance.

❖ **Documentation.** Like anything else, I suppose, some people love to take notes, others don't. If you're in the fortunate position of having one of the former types on your team, count your blessings—let him or her take the minutes and be the official keeper of whatever documentation your group requires.

If not, I've found there are two ways to get this sometimes unpopular task accomplished. One is to rotate responsibility. Each member takes a turn at note taking, publishing the minutes, and so on. That way the task (or pain, depending on your perception) is shared equally among all the members.

The second way is to use a facilitator at meetings. I've found that the team leader or even one of the team members works fine, but, if there is a particularly contentious topic under discussion, it may be useful to use an outside facilitator.

The idea is to have the facilitator "capture" the thoughts and comments on flip chart paper, and then have the sheets transcribed and distributed. One big advantage of this is that everyone can see what's being written, and, if anyone doesn't agree that it's been captured accurately, it can be changed on the spot.

A variation of the flip chart technique is the electronic whiteboard. Thoughts and ideas are captured on the whiteboard and, when the screen is filled, the facilitator simply pushes a button and the image is scanned and printed on the spot. The sheet can then be copied and distributed.

Some people love electronic whiteboards, and they certainly have their benefits. But I'm personally not a fan, mainly because the quality of the output is totally dependent on the quality of the facilitator's handwriting and on his or her ability to organize the thoughts and comments "online" into a logical outline. For most people this is very difficult to do. Another disadvantage is that all the notes are then handwritten, not typed, and the results are not quite as neat and tidy and almost certainly not as easy to read.

Ground Rule: Scope Creep

This is one that usually falls on the shoulders of the team leader, but that isn't necessarily the best way to deal with it. In most cases, virtually every team member is potentially subject to some pressure at some time or other to increase the scope of the undertaking. Usually the pressure comes in the form of innocent-sounding requests, "As long as you're going to be doing 'X' anyway, would you mind just taking a look at 'Y'."

Of course, every time any team member succumbs to these types of requests, a little time and energy is drained from the real project. And yet, for very real and pragmatic reasons, the team doesn't want to get the reputation (either deserved or not) of being uncooperative or unhelpful—after all, they're going to need to rely on assistance from the outside to get their job done.

So what do you do? One of the best ways to handle this is simply to publish—in advance—the team's ground rules regarding scope creep. You may want to wordsmith it to make it more palatable to the outside world, but essentially this accomplishes two purposes. First, it serves notice to everyone that the team is serious about getting its job done, and that it won't be distracted by "out-of-scope" requests. Second, it provides the team with a "fall back position" when confronted with reasonable sounding requests.

When that happens, simply say to the requestor that the team has agreed to bring all such requests to the attention of the entire team so informed decisions can be made. At a minimum, you probably don't want to be in the position of committing the team to do something it's not prepared to do, especially if you're not the one who'll be fulfilling the request. And, there may even be conflicting or overlapping requests to other team members, so it's important everyone be in the loop.

The requestor may not be delighted with this response but, more than likely he or she will understand it. And, after all, you haven't said no, so there's really nothing to be upset about.

So, now that the team has these requests, how do they handle them? My first suggestion is the team ought to comply with any request that doesn't negatively impact the team's performance. The reason, again, is the team will run into unforeseen situations where they will require the assistance of others—it never hurts to have some outstanding "IOU's" to draw on.

But what if you truly cannot do what has been requested? What do you do then? The answer most teams fall back on is the straightforward refusal, couched in a well-rehearsed rationale about why the team doesn't have the time, money, or resources to do what has been requested.

But is this the best response? To understand the answer to that question, let's turn to the Golden Rule. If you were the requestor, what response would you like? How would you like to be treated?

Well, clearly the best answer would be a positive response—one where the team has agreed to do whatever you've asked. But short of that, how would you like to be treated? My guess is that most of us would, at a minimum, like to get some help, even if it isn't everything we've asked for. So, rather than simply saying "no" and explaining why, the team might go back and provide some alternative approaches that might satisfy the essence of what the requestor was looking for, even if it isn't exactly what they asked for.

In other words, my suggestion is to try to provide a positive response to everyone. Those responses fall into four categories:

❖ Say yes. Agree to do whatever has been asked. This one's easy—everybody leaves happy. The requestor gets what he or she wants, and the team gets an "IOU" in the bank.

❖ Provide information. For example, a team member may have a document that would help in some way. Or someone may have special expertise or knowledge that could be relatively quickly communicated.

❖ Provide leads. Even if the team can't help, they may be able to point the requestor in the right direction. The best case would be to provide an introduction to someone who could help.

❖ Offer suggestions. Absent specific help, the team may at least be able to offer some suggestions that may be of benefit to the requestor. At times, even sharing what the team has learned (from either a content or process perspective) may be beneficial.

Ground Rule: Internal and External Communications

Often overlooked, communications—both internal and external—can be a huge factor in determining the team's ultimate success or failure.

❖ **Internal.** The last thing the team wants or needs are issues of trust arising between team members. The best way to avoid this is by constant, open, honest communications. Even *over*-communications. Everyone should keep everyone else informed about what they're doing, the progress they're making, the obstacles they're running into, and the solutions they've devised, and so on.

The question, of course, is how to do that? After all, everyone is busy—in many ways too busy to talk and too busy to listen. But the reality is there's no escape. You ultimately "pay the piper" for breakdowns in communication, and the time and energy spent in repairing the damage will probably take a lot longer than the initial communications would have, had they occurred.

The obvious way to do it is to give an update at team meetings. And that may be enough. But frequent ad hoc communications with team members can also be a major help in several ways. In addition to keeping people informed in the "white space" between team meetings, it helps build relationships and trust between team members, which contribute to camaraderie and team spirit. It inherently prompts reciprocal information sharing, so that the initiator of the communications is not only giving, but also receiving. And it can help surface issues that can then be resolved before they become problems.

❖ **External.** Most teams do a great job of keeping their executive sponsor informed about what they're doing and the progress they're making. They often, however, tend to spend much less time keeping the rest of the organization up to speed.

And yet, oftentimes, it's the "rest of the organization" that is going to determine the team's ultimate success or failure. Keeping interested parties informed should be a key priority of the team, even though it's often viewed as being somewhat extraneous to the team's "real" mission.

So how do you do it? This is as much a cultural as it is a communications issue, so the ultimate answer is very dependent on the organization and the situation. However, there are several possible approaches that may work, given your specific circumstances.

◆ *Focus on the key stakeholders.* First, and most important, identify the key people who have a stake—either positive or negative—in the outcome of your project. Develop a plan to keep these people informed. (The Stakeholder Committee is, of course, the first line of defense here.)

Interestingly, this may be more important for those stakeholders who are inclined to oppose what the team is doing. One approach I've found to be effective is to establish a "win the vote" strategy. Assign specific stakeholders to specific team members, and charge those team members with the responsibility to "win the vote." To overcome opposition. To win friends.

Does it work all the time? Of course not. But it can, I believe, have a positive impact in virtually every case. Remember the Golden Rule. How would you like to be treated if you were a stakeholder? Well, more than likely that's how the stakeholder would like to be treated.

At a minimum, the stakeholder comes to understand that the team truly is concerned about the impact on the stakeholder and his or her organization. It gives the stakeholder an opportunity to express his or her concerns, and the team an opportunity to respond.

In the best of circumstances, the team may be able to address the concerns and convert the stakeholder from an "opposer" to a "supporter" of the team's mission. But even absent that success, they may be able to deflect or mute the stakeholder's opposition.

Some people reject the notion of keeping stakeholders informed the way we've discussed. Their objection is that you're not just supplying them with *information*, you're supplying them with *ammunition*.

I suppose, in a sense, that's true. But the truly antagonistic stakeholder is going to develop his or her own ammunition anyway. Not keeping him or her informed may only add an additional complaint. And by keeping the lines of communication open, you are enhancing your own understanding of the stakeholder's objections, and increasing the odds that you'll be able to deal effectively with them.

This, of course, is a decision each team and each team member must make for themselves. But I believe in general that the merits of sharing outweigh the risks.

♦ *Make everyone a PR Director.* Charge everyone on the team (i.e., Cabinet) with the responsibility for keeping their colleagues, contacts, and constituencies throughout the organization informed about what the team is doing, the progress it's making, the challenges it's facing, and so on. This approach serves two vital purposes. The first is the self-evident one—it keeps people informed.

The second is that it contributes to the building of relationships between team members and the "outside" world. Remember the Golden Rule. How do people on the "outside" want to be treated? Well, by definition, everyone on the team is a "have." They're part of the action. They're "in the know." Nobody wants to be a "have not," yet, if you're not actually a member of the team, you are, by definition, a "have not."

So, frequent communications by each team member to their associates on the outside can help bridge that gap. It can make the outsiders "insiders" at least from a knowledge/information perspective. And that gives these outsiders the additional advantage of knowing something that others don't. Of being "on the inside." Of becoming a "go-to" person when it comes to finding out what's happening. That increases their image and value to the organization, which should increase their appreciation of the team's information sharing.

♦ *Make presentations at other departments' staff meetings.* In most cases, if there are people in other areas in the organization who are interested in the "doings" of a particular team, they'd be more than happy to have a representative of your team present at unit meeting. If you haven't been invited, it may be difficult to wangle an invitation, but it may be worth the effort. A simple comment to the head of the unit stating you'd be happy to stop by and chat—or even present at a meeting—may be all that's required.

♦ *Distribute a "Newsletter."* This is clearly a more formal approach and may, in fact, be done in conjunction with any or all of the other methods. There are also cultural implications to this approach. In some organizations this may be a perfectly acceptable way of communicating. In others it may be seen as overkill or even self-promotion, and may end up having the opposite of the intended effect.

There are also some potential risks. If, for whatever reason, things are not going as well as planned (or hoped), a newsletter may have the effect of exposing you and your efforts to public scrutiny. The public stance implicit in the publishing of such a document may also make it more difficult for you to work through "back channels" to get things done.

Tough issues—decisions only you can make depending on the specific circumstances of your particular situation. If you decide to publish some sort of newsletter, it can be in the form of paper or electronic and should consist of brief updates regarding the team's mission and progress. The tone should be honest and positive and the articles should stick to the facts.

The newsletter should not be used to place public pressure on one or more recalcitrant stakeholders, unless you're prepared to deal with the consequences of such a strategy. Those consequences can include everything from malicious compliance (i.e., living up to the letter of what's been requested, but not the spirit of it), to outright retaliation. Most of us don't need to make enemies—if you have an uncooperative colleague, my suggestion is to stick to more conventional means to garner his or her support.

Whatever choice you make regarding external communications, my suggestion is to make it "official." Assign someone on the team to be the "communications" person—in effect, the team's PR Director.

So there they are—the key "ground rules." Don't make the mistake many teams make and figure you'll handle things as they arise. It's much easier to determine how you're going to deal with these issues "up front" in a detached, unemotional manner, than it is to deal with them when you're "under fire."

Geographically Remote Team Members

Another common situation—and common cause of problems—is having team members who are geographically remote from each other. There is an understandable human tendency to assume that "we're all in this together," and that everybody is "on the same page."

In fact, oftentimes nothing could be further from the truth. The team members back at the "home office" often wonder what their colleagues in the remote locations are doing. Are they, for example, doing their "fair share?" Are they working hard? Are they making progress?

Likewise, remote team members often grumble that the folks back at the home office don't understand their situations. Don't appreciate what they're going through. Try to impose ill-fitting solutions for problems at the remote sites that they don't understand. And, in general, take a dictatorial "I'm from headquarters; I'm here to help" attitude.

So who's right? Well, as in most situations involving human beings, the answer is far from clear. But, in my experience, both sides are typically a little bit right and a little bit wrong. So what do you do? Well, the answer must be obvious by now—invoke the Golden Rule. Team members on both sides should treat the others the way they would like to be treated.

Would you, for example, if you were remote, like to be dictated to? Or treated in a condescending manner by headquarters "do-gooders?"

Or, on the other hand, if you were from the home office, would you like to be kept in the dark about what's going on in the remote locations? Or, as sometimes happens, treated like "the enemy" when you visit remote colleagues?

Of course not, is the answer to all those questions, so don't treat other people that way. I've found that the following tool is a helpful reminder of the key leverage points in working effectively in situations where there are remote team members. It's an acronym, and, as with most tools like this, there's a message in the acronym itself. The acronym is CALLER-RT, and it implies that, since "in-person" meetings are probably relatively infrequent, frequent telephone communications are critical.

Communicate. Often. Talk to each other. Try to emulate the experience of physically working together, where frequent "hallway" or "water cooler" conversations are common. Call each other just to "check in," see how things are going, share experiences. Make these frequent calls one of the team's ground rules so people don't wonder if there's an ulterior motive if people are "checking *up* on," and not just checking *in* on.

Assumptions. Don't make them. When in doubt (as to whether something is an assumption or a fact) try to validate it one way or the other. How? First, simply ask the question: Is this an assumption or is it a fact? If it's an assumption, I've found the best way to validate or invalidate it is simply to ask. Plus, you get the added benefit of an opportunity for enhanced communications.

Learn. Don't assume you know what's best. Try to understand what's really going on in the other locations. What the real issues, challenges, and strains are. How? By periodically visiting. By talking to people. By keeping a sharp ear tuned. By not assuming. By being willing to learn.

Let Go. Within the overall context of achieving the vision, give the people who know the situation best the authority to deal with it in the way they believe to be best. Don't assume you know better than they do. And this applies to both the remote and home office groups. The remote folks, for example, may believe their situation is so different that certain elements of the vision don't (or can't) apply to them. But the folks at the home office may believe a consistent application of certain elements is critical to the success of the vision. Both groups need to "test" those beliefs and be willing to listen and learn—and "give" where it makes sense for the overall good of the vision.

Enjoy. Everybody works hard these days. Probably harder than they did five years ago. And they worked harder five years ago than they did five years before that. If we don't find a way to enjoy what we're doing, it becomes a "quality of life" issue. Not only does it affect our performance—even potentially our judgment when it comes to things like the vision—but it affects our personal lives as well.

Relationships. How many times have we used that word already? Business is a people game. It's all about relationships. The more relationships you build, and the better those relationships are, the easier—and more fun—your job will be.

Respect. It's true people have to earn respect—it's not necessarily something that's bestowed on them. But there's certainly no harm in going into situations and relationships with an attitude of respect. If it's not deserved, that will become clear soon enough. But better to start that way and potentially have to re-evaluate than to begin with a lack of respect that can hinder effective communications and relationship building.

Trust. This is probably one of the most important elements of not only working effectively across remote geographies, but of working effectively, period. There's a neat equation that I find useful when it comes to building trust—you may find it useful as well. The equation is:

$$\text{Trust} = \frac{\text{Authenticity} \times \text{Credibility} \times \text{Relationship}}{\text{Risk}^2}$$

Authenticity means you are who you seem to be. You are honest and forthright in your dealings with others. If there is self-interest, as well as mutual interest involved, you're open about it, so it doesn't seem as though you're trying to "put one over on" your colleague(s). You can be relied on to "be yourself," and, in that sense, people will be able to develop a comfort level regarding how you will respond to given situations.

Credibility means you can be relied on to live up to your commitments. You say what you mean and you do what you say. You "deliver."

Relationship is just what you assume it means. You have developed a human bond of some sort. It doesn't imply you are necessarily "bosom buddies," rather it suggests that you develop rapport and "share and care" with each other, and that sharing and caring extends beyond simple business issues and into personal issues. The strength of the relationship is probably more a function of how deeply connected you are at the personal level than at the business level.

Risk^2 suggests two types of risk: personal and business. Personal, in this sense, means as it applies to your business life—job, career, opportunities for advancement, compensation, and so on. Business risk is just what it says—the potential downside from a business perspective.

So, if you want to build trust: Be authentic, build credibility, build the relationship, and do everything possible to minimize risk, both from a personal and business perspective.

Team Success Elements

Talk to managers, executives, and professionals and they can all outline the key elements necessary for a team to be successful. It's not rocket science, and it's not a secret.

Yet, as we noted earlier, these same executives, managers, and professionals, when asked to evaluate the performance of teams they've been on, rated the performance at only about six on a scale of one to ten.

So, the logical questions are: What are these "success elements?" And why do teams have such difficulty in following this "formula?" As to the first question, here's what the folks we talk to tell us:

Team Success Elements

Mission. The team must have a clear mission and everyone on the team must understand what that mission is. They must "buy-into" it and fully support it.

The "Right" People on the Team. People with the necessary knowledge and skills, and individuals who have the authority to make the decisions that must be made.

Goals/Objectives. The mission must be broken down into a set of clearly defined goals/objectives that, again, everyone must understand and agree to.

Roles and Responsibilities. Everyone on the team must clearly understand what is expected, not only of them, but of the other team members as well.

Commitment. Team members must be committed to the mission, and must be willing to contribute their maximum effort to accomplish that mission.

Trust. Team members must trust each other. This applies not only to the obvious issue of getting the job done, but to deeper issues like "trusting" there are no hidden agendas, that team members won't "backstab" each other, won't seek individual recognition at the expense of the team, and so on.

Effective Communications. Team members must communicate effectively with each other and, both individually and as a group, with people outside the team.

Good Working Relationships. Team members must have good interpersonal skills, must be able to get along with each other, and work effectively together.

There's probably nothing in the above list that surprises anyone. It's all relatively straightforward and seemingly easy to implement. So why the disconnect? Why is it that intelligent, hard-working, dedicated professionals are not able to translate their knowledge into performance?

We've found that there are several reasons, all of which are surprisingly simple. Oftentimes it's as simple as confusing a *committee* with a *team* (as we've previously defined them). That's relatively easy to correct—break the committee into smaller groups who can operate as teams.

Sometimes it's as simple as "multiple different" interpretations of the mission. People implicitly assume that everyone on the team understands the mission and will work diligently to accomplish it. But if everyone is working diligently in pursuit of different missions, it's very difficult to make progress. The solution: Make the implicit explicit. Ensure everyone not only has an understanding of the mission, but that everyone has the *same* understanding.

But trust is probably the biggest "under-miner" of team success. People intuitively know you can't walk into a roomful of people and have everyone automatically trust each other. Trust takes time to establish. It means building relationships. Building credibility. All the things we stated earlier.

And yet trust is also easily broken, and once it's broken, it's very difficult to mend. It's one of the "unspokens" in business. Trust issues are more often the result of innocent misunderstandings than malicious intent. And once trust (or, more precisely the lack of trust) rears its ugly head, it's very difficult to overcome.

The one who is mistrusted may not even realize it, particularly if the trigger of the mistrust was, in fact, something innocent and unintended. And the "mistruster" will almost never confront the person he or she mistrusts. Very rarely in business (or in life, for that matter) will you hear anyone say to someone, "I don't trust you." As a result, the issue simmers beneath the surface, undermines the efforts of the team, and saps it of its energy.

So what do you do? First, I believe, it's important to recognize that trust issues are almost certainly going to arise, and if and when they do, they will drain the team of its productive potential. Therefore, understanding that people will be reluctant to surface these disabling issues, an explicit plan must be put in place to deal with them.

How to Deal With "Trust" Issues

I've found there are four ground rules that make it somewhat less painful to surface and discuss trust issues.

1. Accept the fact that trust issues are a normal part of doing business, and make that acceptance a group norm so team members are more comfortable addressing the issues. Maybe even make it a ground rule.

2. Assume the trust issue was created by an innocent misunderstanding rather than by malicious intent.

3. Use non-accusatory language. For example, don't say, "He, she, or you did such and such…." Rather, use language like, "It's my perception that…."

4. Agree to use the discussion as a learning experience for the future, rather than as a criticism of past behaviors.

With these ground rules in place, I've found that people are quite capable of objectively and unemotionally surfacing trust issues, determining why the issue arose, and deciding on future courses of action that will prevent them from recurring.

Step 3: Assemble the Team—Key Points Summary

A. A two-tier "team" structure is useful in supporting your efforts to accomplish the vision.

    1. The *Cabinet* consists of a small group of trusted advisors, all of whom fully support the vision.

    2. The *Stakeholder Committee* consists of key stakeholders who will be impacted—either positively or negatively—by your efforts to accomplish the vision. This can include representatives from human resources, finance, information technology and other areas.

B. The role of the Cabinet is to:

    1. Enthusiastically support and promote the vision.

    2. Participate in the development of a high-level agenda to accomplish the vision.

3. Define roles and responsibilities for members of the Cabinet and diligently perform any assigned tasks.

4. "Sell" the vision to stakeholders.

5. Motivate employees to enthusiastically support the vision and engage in efforts to achieve it.

C. The role of the Stakeholder Committee is to:

1. Learn about your efforts to achieve the vision.

2. Share issues, concerns, and problems with the vision and your efforts to achieve the vision.

3. Cooperate with you to resolve those potential obstacles to success. This may include suggesting alternative approaches that may help avoid problems.

D. There are four major reasons teams are not as effective as they could be:

1. "Teams" are often too big—tending to be more of a committee than a team. Six to eight members seems to be about the right number.

2. Teams often fail to establish a set of working "ground rules."

3. Members are often geographically remote from each other.

4. Teams often fail to execute an effective "team process" that will lead to high performance.

E. Ground rules that cover the following areas should be established upfront:

1. Poor performance.

2. Team dynamics.

3. Scope creep.

4. Internal and external communications.

F. When teams have members who are geographically remote from each other, there are some important points to keep in mind that can help ensure effective performance:

Communicate—with each other.

Assumptions—validate them.

Learn—from each other.

Let go—be willing to let those closest to the issues/problems handle them.

Enjoy—life is too short, and we work too hard. We've got to find a way to enjoy what we do.

Relationships—build them, nurture them.

Respect—each other.

Trust—each other.

G. Trust is a function of authenticity, credibility, relationships, and risk (both personal and business). When trust issues arise, there are some simple ground rules that can facilitate dealing with them:

1. Accept—as a group norm—that trust issues are a normal part of doing business.

2. Assume the trust issue was created by an innocent misunderstanding rather than by malicious intent.

3. Use non-accusatory language.

4. Use the discussion as a learning experience for the future, rather than as a criticism of past behaviors.

H. To be most effective, teams must follow an approach that incorporates the following elements:

- Mission
- "Right" People
- Goals/Objectives
- Roles and Responsibilities
- Commitment
- Trust
- Effective Communications
- Good Working Relationships

Pathway to Success
The Golden Rule and the
Leadership Process

Step 4: Set the Agenda

To be prepared is half the victory.

Miguel de Cervantes

First, I want to be very specific about this. An "agenda," in the context in which we're using the term here, is not a "plan," not a detailed outline of what has to be done to accomplish the vision. It's a high-level overview of the key areas that must be addressed if the vision is to be achieved.

So what are those areas? Perhaps the best way to introduce them is by way of example, introduced by the following "fiction based on fact" case study.

Cookie Burke[5]

"Cookie" Burke was concerned. He was going over the numbers for his diner with his accountant "Shades" Logan, an old army buddy, and realized things weren't looking too good. Cookie couldn't quite figure out why and Shades wasn't much help.

"Maybe you should sell the place," Shades said. "Or at least think about it. Right now it probably still has some value—who knows what it's going to look like in six months or a year."

The Place

"The place" was Cookie's Diner. Cookie bought it in 1946, not too long after he was discharged from the army after having served with distinction as a cook with Colonel Abrams' 37th Tank Battalion in Europe. The first ten or twelve years had been great. Located outside Providence on the Boston Post Road (or Route 1, as it was officially named), "Cookie's" (as everyone called it) literally had more business than it could handle. In fact, in order to make sure he could serve all his customers, Cookie had instituted a rigorous set of rules—mainly having to do with customers.

For example, they had to wait to be seated, that way Cookie made sure he filled all his seats. No twosomes at a table for four. No singles at a table at all, they had to sit at the counter. And, perhaps most important of all, NO SUBSTITU-TIONS. Cookie had put together what he thought was a great menu. Good food (he did all the cooking himself). Good selection and reasonable combinations of entrees, potatoes, and vegetables. There was no need for anyone to substitute any-thing.

And besides, if he let them do that, it would mess up everything in his kitchen. After so many years of experience, he knew pretty well how many Number One's and Number Two's and so on, that would sell on any given day, and how many specials went on Wednesdays, and how many All-American Breakfast Combo Platters went on Saturday mornings. That meant he knew just what to order and in what quantities. And, he had his whole kitchen layout arranged to make it easy to prepare meals according to his numbering system.

And it worked. In fact, it worked great! Cookie knew that all the diners did it essentially the same way. He knew that because he had taken the time to stop in at a couple places up and down the Post Road—there was a diner about thirty-five or forty miles away in each direction—it took a while but, other than that, it was relatively easy to check them out.

The Customers

By now, Cookie's regular customers were all "trained." The only ones who asked for substitutions at this point were the ones who hadn't been there before. And Cookie made sure his waitresses rigorously enforced the "no substitutions" policy. Customers who pressed too hard on that point were apt to be shown the door—and none too gently either. Cookie smiled as he thought about those two scruffy-looking kids who had stopped in on their way to Boston a few months ago. They gave Flo a hard time, and she gave them the boot—and good riddance as far as Cookie was concerned.

The Good Old Days

But those were the good old days. Recently, during the past year or so, things had started to change. The build-up of the nationwide highway system that Eisenhower began a few years before had caught up to New England, and there wasn't as much traffic on the Post Road anymore. And less traffic meant fewer customers.

Moreover, another one of his army buddies, a cook who had also bought a diner, but closer to Boston, was complaining about these new hamburger joints that were popping up all over the place. Said it was killing his business. Cookie couldn't understand that. The food wasn't just cheap (or inexpensive as the hamburger joints liked to say), it was just plain lousy as far as Cookie was concerned. And all you could get was a burger and fries! Certainly no competition for the vast menu and good cooking he offered his customers.

Back to the Future

But, whatever it was, the numbers didn't lie. Cookie's Diner was actually on the verge of losing money—and it didn't look like things were going to get better anytime soon. Cookie was trying to figure out what he could do to rejuvenate his business, but he was also beginning to wonder whether Shades was right after all—maybe he should sell.

What Should Cookie Do?

So, what should Cookie do? Rather than try to answer that outright, let's begin by exploring his options. He could continue to do what he's always done—continue to operate the same way. That's one option. Or he could take Shades' advice and sell. That's a second option.

Or he could try to do things differently. Try to rejuvenate the business based on the changes that were taking place in the environment. That's his third option.

Of course, there are probably virtually an infinite variety of other things Cookie could do, but they would basically fall within one of these three categories, so let's examine each of these in turn.

Option 1: Continue to operate the way he always has

Einstein's definition of insanity was continuing to do things the same way and expecting to get a different result. So, if Cookie continues to operate the same way, more than likely he will continue to get the same result. That is, a continuing decline in customers, revenue and income. Probably not the best option for Cookie. (Yet, incredibly enough, this is the very route that many—if not most—diners actually took. And, with the benefit of hindsight, we know what a mistake this was—by the late sixties/early seventies some eighty percent of the diners that existed in the early fifties had gone out of business.)

Option 2: Sell out

This is what Shades thinks Cookie should do, and he may be right. But there are some issues. What's the market like? After all, the diner "industry" is clearly suffering at this point in time. And what's Cookie going to do if he sells out? He's probably too young to retire, and probably couldn't get enough for his diner to do that anyway.

One variation of this option, of course, is for Cookie to sell out and then use the proceeds from the sale to buy a franchise in one of these new "hamburger joints." In retrospect, that may have been the best option for diner owners, perhaps including Cookie. But, for purposes of our discussion, let's assume he chooses option three, rejuvenate the business.

Option 3: Rejuvenate the business: Do things differently

This is the option we really want to focus on. It gets at the question of "agenda." And it is a direct application of the GRL. If you really want to lead change, what sorts of things—at a high level—do you need to be concerned about? What sorts of things do you want your "team" to focus on? How would you like to be treated if you were an employee or a potential customer?

Let's assume Cookie recognizes the challenge. He realizes he's lost his primary customer set—that is, the traveling public—to the restaurants located on the new super-highways. And he determines he doesn't want to compete with the "fast-food" outfits, which service the needs of customers looking for a fast, cheap meal. Rather, Cookie decides he wants to become a destination outlet—that he specifically wants to attract people to his diner for breakfast, lunch and dinner. What does he have to do? How would customers of this type of a destination outlet like to be treated?

Well, since his "vision" is to become a destination outlet, the first question is, what do people look for in such a place—how do they want to be treated? In effect, what changes would he have to make?

In official "business" terms, Cookie's Diner always operated as a "product-focused" business. The implicit message was, "Here's what we serve, and how we serve it. If that's what you want, fine. If not, go someplace else." And that's exactly the way the waiters and waitresses behaved.

But think Golden Rule. If you were a customer, is this how you would like to be treated? If Cookie wants to transform his operation and attract customers, he's got to shift to a more customer-oriented model, which means he has to fundamentally rethink the way he does business.

For example, the "wait staff" has to be retrained. Their mission is no longer to "provide product," but to "serve customers." So the implicit question is not, "Do you want this or not," it's "What can I get for you?" And that question must be relayed to the customer in a friendly, courteous manner. That implies a dramatic shift in attitude from what we saw in the case study. (For Cookie as well as the wait staff, since he is clearly of the same mindset as they.)

And it's not just attitude, it's time as well. It will probably take longer to provide this kind of "customer-friendly" service. So Cookie may have to add staff, which means scheduling will become more complicated, managing the employees will take more time and energy, and costs will go up.

Perhaps most importantly from Cookie's perspective, if he really wants to attract customers the "no substitutions" policy will have to go and the menu may have to change to allow more flexibility in ordering. (Again, think Golden Rule. If you were a customer wouldn't you want some choice in your meal selection?)

That means things have to change both upstream and downstream from the ordering process. For example, Cookie has to be prepared to satisfy an unknown number of requests for unknown quantities of a wide variety of foods. That means the ordering process will change and inventories will increase, which means the cost of purchasing and carrying product will go up. Spoilage will almost certainly increase—since it will be more difficult to plan accurately—which means those costs will go up.

Even the layout of the kitchen and the meal preparation process may have to change. In the past, Cookie could keep the components of the most frequently ordered dishes together and in close proximity to the cooking equipment. Now he may have to inventory the food by type rather than by meal.

All this uncertainty around costs means Cookie will have to rethink his prices—they'll almost certainly have to increase. And that takes us full circle—customers are certainly not going to be willing to pay more to get the same dining experience, so all those other changes we mentioned become even more important.

Of course, all these changes won't mean much if nobody (i.e., potential customers) is aware of them. So Cookie also has to design, develop and implement a marketing plan that will communicate the "new" Cookie's Diner to the target market.

I realize we've probably only scratched the surface with this analysis of Cookie's Diner. But I do think it serves to illustrate the complexity and difficulty of making change in any organization, even one as seemingly straightforward as a diner.

Now imagine your own situation, which is probably much more complex and much less straightforward than the example we used. Certainly, almost assuredly, completely different. So what relevance does Cookie's Diner have?

"Pyramiding" the Changes

That's where frameworks and methodologies can be so helpful. Let's take another brief look at Cookie's—this time from the perspective of "pyramiding" the changes that Cookie may have to make so we can create a short list of generic items that anyone in any organization contemplating change may have to consider.

❖ *Vision* is the first thing that strikes us. When contemplating change, we have to know not only what we're changing from, but also what we're changing to. Here, all the things we stated in Chapter 2 come into play. It must be (1) memorable, (2) clear, concise, and unambiguous, (3) personal, (4) motivational, (5) positive, (6) unifying, (7) inclusive, and (8) unencumbered with details. I suppose we could go back and stack Cookie's vision of becoming a "destination outlet" up against this list. But a quick glance is probably enough to tell us that basically he has captured the essence of these things.

And we have to remember the Golden Rule. People who will be asked to support the vision will want to know what that vision is. Where is the leader planning on taking them? So the communication of that vision is critically important also.

❖ Cookie also made some fundamental changes in *strategy*. Shifting from being product-focused to customer-focused is probably the most overarching example. But there are others. Pricing, for one thing. Marketing, for another.

Again, think Golden Rule. If you were a potential customer, how would you like to be treated? What sources of information would you investigate before making a "dining out" decision? How would you evaluate "price" in relation to other variables that impact your choice of restaurant?

❖ Changes in *processes* may also be required. In Cookie's case, those were relatively straightforward. The customer seating process. The ordering process. The cooking process and so on.

It's probably a lot more complex in most organizations today. But the basic issue is the same. If you're changing strategy, you probably need to rethink your basic processes as well. Procurement, operations, marketing, sales, customer service, and so on—all need to be re-examined to ensure they are relevant and viable given the new strategy.

And rethinking processes means applying the Golden Rule. If you were a participant in a process that was going to be changed as a result of changes in strategy, wouldn't you want to participate in the "process" that would determine what those changes needed to be? After all, you and your colleagues "on the line" would know more about that process than anyone else. You would know where the "land mines" and "pitfalls" are. What the "work-arounds" are. Wouldn't you feel you could make a valuable contribution, and wouldn't you want to be involved?

❖ A fourth major area is *structure*. Cookie may have to "renovate" the organizational structure. Maybe he needs to create—and fill—the position of an assistant manager or even one or more "crew chiefs." That, of course, will impact reporting relationships. Instead of reporting directly to the owner, employees now will be one or two levels removed from the "big boss." A significant loss of stature and prestige.

So, of course, the Golden Rule comes into play. But how? If the changes have to be made, they have to be made. What does it matter whether you pay attention to the Golden Rule or not?

Well, remember, all the Golden Rule says is you should treat people the way you would like to be treated. In this case, if there is no choice, if these organizational changes must be made regardless of how people feel about them, then, at a minimum, we need to be sensitive to how they (the employees who are being impacted) feel about them.

It's not just some boxes on a sheet of paper. It's a big part of their lives. Their position at work can potentially impact their self-image, their self-esteem, their self-confidence, and possibly a number of other "self" things.

So, if the employees can't be involved in the decision-making process, at least keep them informed. Communicate. Over-communicate. Explain the situation. Explain what's driving the need for change. And explain the rationale around the decisions that have been made.

But first, test your conclusion that they can't be involved in the decision-making process. I submit to you that there are ways in which they could be. Ways that could facilitate the process and ease the transition.

For example, after explaining the situation (as described above) you could potentially—in either a figurative or in an actual sense—remove people from their current positions (to eliminate vested interests and jockeying for position), form teams, and ask the employees to make suggestions about an organization structure that would met the needs you've outlined. You could even potentially ask them for recommendations as to whom should fill which "boxes" on the chart. (For example, you could form logical work groups and ask those groups to pick their own "team leader.")

There's a common concern on the part of "management" that, given an opportunity like that, all the employees would place themselves at the top of the pyramid. But I've found that's not the case. Many employees, for example, don't want to be the "boss." They don't want the responsibility or the "headaches." Others who may want the job may recognize that they're not quite ready for it. That they need additional "seasoning" or training.

And almost everyone will have pretty strong opinions about who should fill those slots. They have a pretty good idea about who would make a good boss and who wouldn't. Who they'd like to work for, and who they wouldn't. Who would motivate them, and who wouldn't.

And they're probably right. And, to the degree that you can implement their suggestions, you can ease the transition to the new structure.

❖ There are potentially a myriad of changes required in *systems* as well. Inventory is one example, as we discussed. But also compensation, incentive and reward systems. While it wasn't true in Cookie's day (at least not universally true), today information systems are a key consideration of any change process.

And changes in systems—like changes in organizations—can have a dramatic impact on people and their jobs. The "go-to" person, for example, who is a "whiz" at pulling together data and compiling reports, may be replaced by a computer specialist who knows how to manage a new information system where those same reports—or improved, more flexible versions of them—can be pulled together faster, cheaper and easier.

If you were that "go-to" person, how would you like to be treated? At a minimum, wouldn't you want to be kept informed about what was happening? What changes were afoot? What those changes would mean to you and your job. And wouldn't you want to have an opportunity to learn the new system, make the transition, and maintain your status?

Of course you would. So treat other people the same way. Involve them in the process that will result in the installation of these new systems. Give them an opportunity to change along with the systems. To learn the new way. To maintain their positions as valued members of the team.

❖ *Staffing* was a critical issue for Cookie, and is one of the key considerations in virtually all change initiatives. Do you have the right number of people? In the right positions? Do they have the necessary skills, knowledge and attitude?

I know this is beating the drum, but I think it's important to keep it in mind. If you're thinking about staff changes, think Golden Rule. How would you like to be treated? If you were an employee, and new knowledge and skills were required for success in a changed environment, wouldn't you want an opportunity to acquire those rather than being looked over because you don't have them today?

Or, if new positions are being created, wouldn't you want an opportunity to compete for them? The issue is the same—treat people the way you would like to be treated. It's not just a better way to treat people. It's a better way to run a business.

❖ Finally, *culture*. In Cookie's case, the change was dramatic. For others, the question is what will you value—as an organization—in the new world, versus what you valued in the old? How important are customers? How important is quality? How important—in a relative sense—are costs? Service? Speed? And so on.

And how do you want people to relate to each other within the organization? Some organizations value politeness. Others directness. Some even value internal contention, believing it contributes to creativity and innovation. What's important to you?

What sorts of "things" do you want to do to support the vision? What sorts of awards and recognition do you want to put in place? How do you want to "socialize" the vision? What examples do you want to share that support the new direction?

Just as importantly, what's important to the people in your organization? Remember, culture, for the most part, isn't created "on-high" and *imposed* on an organization. If anything, it develops from below and merely surfaces upon inspection. As in the above areas, but perhaps even more so here, losing sight of the Golden Rule can cost you. In a sense, the people in the organization "own" the culture. How they behave toward each other, the stories they tell around the water cooler, what they value, and how they have fun—that *is* the culture.

And no one can come in and simply wave some sort of organizational "magic wand" and change all that. If it's going to change, it's going to change because the people cause it to change—or at least believe in the change enough to let it happen.

Well, there it is. That's your agenda. These are the things you need to be thinking about when launching any sort of change process. And, as we noted earlier, leadership is fundamentally about people and change.

We can lay this out in a somewhat easier to remember framework to aid in developing the necessary follow-on plans.

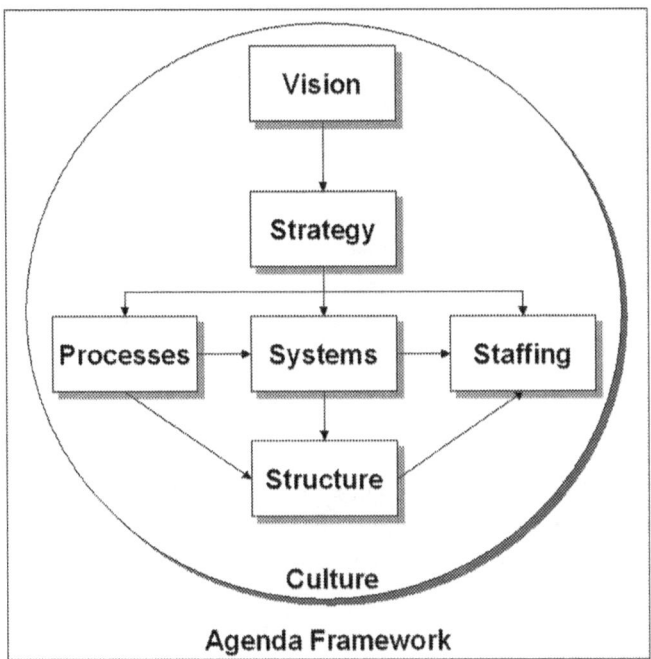

Agenda Framework

Vision

Vision comes first. That's the driver of the change process. You have to know where you're going before you can embark on a journey of change. As we noted earlier, it doesn't have to be on the scale of "send a man to the moon," but it does have to give people a sense of where they're headed, and what the final outcome will be.

Strategy

A new vision suggests the need to rethink, and possibly (or even probably), change strategy. If you want to change as an organization, which is what a new vision implies, you almost certainly are going to have to change what you're doing, and how you're operating. To repeat: Einstein's definition of insanity is continuing to do things the same way and expecting to get a different result. If we want a different result, we must do things differently.

Processes

The old saying that structure follows strategy is true as far as it goes, but it is incomplete. The reality is that structure follows process, which follows strategy. Once you have developed your strategy, the next challenge is to put the necessary processes in place to enable you to successfully execute that strategy. Some existing processes may stay the same, some may change, and you may have to introduce some new processes. There is a variety of mechanisms that will allow you to determine which processes fall within which categories, but the critical thing is to avoid the mistake of assuming existing business processes will somehow just conform to the new strategy. They must be examined and examined carefully.

Systems

Systems are kind of the "glue" that holds everything together. They're integral to virtually everything that's done in an organization today, and so impact—or are impacted by—changes in strategy and processes.

Structure

Once your processes have been established, it's possible to take a look at structure. It's important to understand who's performing what tasks and procedures within the processes, within what functional areas they currently reside, and whether or not they should stay there.

The potential that structure may change, in and of itself, explains why change is so difficult in organizations. Structure defines turf. Turf, in many organizations, defines power. If you change the structure, by definition, you impact turf and power. And that, of course, means some people are going to be helped, and some are going to be hurt. The ones who sense they may be hurt are going resist the change, and probably vigorously resist it.

(That's why it's so important to have "assembled your team," and to have an overarching "agenda." It allows you to anticipate where the trouble spots may be, and to assign a trusted team member to deal with whatever that trouble may be. In advance. Before the resistance has an opportunity to "circle the wagons" and hinder your efforts to implement necessary improvements.)

Staffing

If you're making changes in strategy, processes, structure and systems, almost certainly you will need to make "staffing" changes. The first of those changes is probably in the definitions of the jobs themselves. If, for example, you're going to change a process, you are, by definition going to change the nature (and, therefore, the definition) of the jobs related to that process. If you change job definitions, you're going to need to rethink the knowledge and skills required to do those re-defined jobs. That means you're going to have to review the current knowledge and skills of existing employees to see if they will be able to discharge the responsibilities of the re-defined jobs. Conclusions related to that analysis might suggest a need for re-training, redeployment or replacement.

Anyway, you get the idea. Staffing is a critical area that needs to be examined.

Culture

Finally, culture. So elusive a concept, and yet so powerful a force. You can "get away with" almost anything in an organization except "messing with" the culture. And yet it's virtually impossible to precisely define just what culture, in general, is and, perhaps more importantly, what a specific organization's culture is.

But let's try—let's try to develop a list of key parameters that help to define culture, so we can at least be aware of how our change initiative may impact those parameters.

One is **values**. Every organization values something—either implicitly or explicitly. Toyota values quality. Wal-Mart values customer service. Southwest Airlines values employees. And so on. That doesn't mean that's the only thing those companies value—it just means it's a key variable in their decision-making process. At Toyota the key question is, how will a given change impact quality? If the answer is that it will have a positive impact on quality, that change has the potential of moving forward. If not, it will probably be "killed" (in an organizational sense).

Likewise for Wal-Mart and Southwest Airlines. Changes that positively impact customer service and employee satisfaction, respectively, may move forward. Changes that have the potential for negative impacts probably won't make it.

A second parameter is **interpersonal style**. How do people relate to each other? How do they deal with each other?

At one large company with which we've worked, the interpersonal style is politeness. The answer "yes" is a polite way of acknowledging that someone has told you something, has relayed information. It does not imply agreement or support—those must be explicitly stated. Woe be unto the outsider—at any level, but particularly at higher levels—who joins the organization and does not understand that cultural parameter. It's been the cause of many a fall from grace.

At another, the style is directness. To some on the outside looking in, it may appear to be abruptness, or even rudeness. But it works for this company. And their style helps them—as it does the "polite" company's style—get things done.

A third parameter is **socializing**. How does the company socialize at work, and in company related "after-work" events, like holiday parties? IBM, for example, has long been known for the more sedate, formal style of celebration. For a long time, drinking—even possession of alcoholic beverages on IBM premises—was grounds for immediate dismissal. Contrast that with many of the upstart Silicon Valley high-tech companies, for many of whom the Friday afternoon party has become almost an entitlement.

Rewards/recognition is the fourth parameter. How does the company celebrate success, for example? Are there public meetings where honors are bestowed, or is it done more on an individual basis? Do the rewards/recognition tend to be monetary or non-monetary (e.g., vacation trips or merchandise)? At Toyota, for example, the cultural "badge of honor" is a certificate hung in a work area.

And the final parameter is **folklore**. What do people talk about around the water cooler and during lunch? At Federal Express they tell heroic stories, like couriers renting helicopters and flying to remote locations in blizzards to deliver packages on time. At Southwest Airlines they tell funny stories about the latest antics of this flight attendant, or that agent, that got customers laughing. At Nordstrom's they tell stories of dedication and determination—how a shoe salesperson, for example, when faced with an out-of-stock situation, asked the customer to wait for a moment, ran to a nearby store, purchased the product and brought it back and sold it to his customer at a price lower than what he had paid. All positive, uplifting stories that tend to help define the nature of the company, and the nature of the people it employs.

Not every company, of course, is fortunate enough to have developed this type of positive, "can-do" culture. But these types of stories can be an important way to facilitate that process. And celebrations—particularly of the types of successes that the company wants to see emulated throughout the organization—can help to spawn those stories.

So, the question for us, is how will the change we're promoting impact these variables: values, interpersonal style, socializing, rewards/recognition and folklore? If the impact is positive, the change initiative will probably "go" much more smoothly. If negative, it may not "go" at all.

So there we have it, the framework for building the overarching "change" agenda: vision, strategy, processes, structure, systems, staffing and culture. Each of these areas needs to be carefully thought through in order to ensure the highest probability of success for the change initiative.

Keys to Success

The question, of course, is what, specifically, does it mean to "think these areas through?" Primarily, it means two things. First, understanding who will be impacted by the change (i.e., who the stakeholders are), determining what their current position is regarding the change (i.e., positive, negative or neutral), and developing a plan to:

1. Reinforce the positives;

2. Maintain the neutrals, or perhaps move them into the positive column; and,

3. Convert the negatives to neutrals, or even to positives, or, failing that, at least minimize their ability to obstruct the change process.

The chart below may be a helpful way to capture those plans. This type of analysis can give you an "at-a-glance" perspective to ensure you've included all the critical functional areas on your team. In fact, it may even be helpful in determining who you want to invite on your team (i.e., Cabinet and Stakeholder Committee) to help lead the change process.

Stakeholder Name	Functional Area of Responsibility	How Stakeholder Can Help/Hurt Effort	Current Attitude Toward Change Initiative	Actions to be Taken

Stakeholder Analysis Tool

Secondly, it means really energizing the employees. Getting them engaged in the overall process. Making them a part of the successful achievement of the vision. We'll address each of these two areas—i.e., stakeholders and employees—in the next two steps of the Leadership Process.

Step 4: Set the Agenda—Key Points Summary

A. An "agenda" is a high-level overview of the key areas which must be addressed if the vision is to be achieved; not a detailed outline of the specific actions that must be taken.

B. At a minimum, the agenda should address the following areas: vision, strategy, processes, structure, systems, staffing and culture.

C. Culture is defined by the organization's values, interpersonal style, celebrations and rituals, and the stories people tell.

D. In addressing the areas on the agenda, there are two keys to success: analyzing the stakeholders and energizing the employees.

Pathway to Success
The Golden Rule and the
Leadership Process

Step 5: Engage the Stakeholders

If you want to build a ship, don't drum up people together
to collect wood and don't assign them tasks and work, but rather teach them
to long for the endless immensity of the sea.

Antoine de Saint-Exupery

In the next chapter we'll discuss the whole critical issue of energizing employees. Here we're addressing a related, but different issue—that of engaging other functional areas outside your sphere of control, in your efforts to launch and successfully complete a change initiative.

As we stated earlier, the days of rugged individualism are long gone, if indeed, they were really ever here. Today, in order to be successful, you must rely on the efforts not only of the people within your organizational unit, but also people outside the boundaries of your area of responsibility.

That means you cannot use authority to get things done. You must, instead, rely on personal influence.

So the question before us is, how do we increase our own personal influence (and, therefore, power) throughout the organization?

In workshops we hold to address this particular question, we run participants through a simulated business situation. The exercise creates an environment where separate teams are established and asked to resolve a resource issue that has significant implications for each individual team, and for the group as a whole.

Results are measured both on the absolute performance of the total group, and on the relative performance of each of the individual teams. In order to maximize both overall and individual team performance, the teams must find a way to work together.

Initially, teams tend to operate in their own self-interest. For the most part, each team plays its cards "close to the vest." As time goes on, teams that are not faring too well, become much more willing to "deal." But teams that are doing better, tend to try and maximize their own positions first, and then carefully—and usually very reluctantly—attempt to help as they become convinced of the needs articulated by the other teams.

No group has ever "max'd out" on the scoring system. Very few groups have even come close. For the most part, they end up getting about half to two-thirds of the way there. Why is that? Even though it is quite clear in the information that's provided to them that the best way to maximize not only the overall score, but also their own team score, is by cooperating, why is it that teams simply don't want to do that?

The four primary causes of dysfunctional cross-organizational relationships

We've identified four major reasons: assumptions, trust, communication and focus. Let's examine each in more detail.

1. **Assumptions.** Virtually every team goes into the exercise making several assumptions. Assumptions about the condition of the other teams—how well or bad off they are. Assumptions about the "motivation" of the other teams—are they really working for the overall good of the entire group, or are they trying to maximize their own positions. Assumptions about the scoring structure, even about the "rules" of the exercise.

   Most often the assumptions that are made are not only incorrect, but are in conflict with other incorrect assumptions made by other teams. You can imagine the confusion, withdrawal and mistrust that are engendered by the behaviors resulting from these mistaken and divergent assumptions.

   And yet, in virtually every case these assumptions could have easily been validated or invalidated by asking a few simple questions. But, in the vast majority of exercises that we hold, they are, instead, treated as facts by the participants. Rarely does anyone take the time to—or even think to—validate them.

2. **Trust.** The second major reason teams don't cooperate well is trust. Regardless of how well participants know each other, and regardless of how,

during previous discussions, they may have emphasized how well they work together internally, when it comes right down to it during the exercise, for the most part they simply don't trust each other.

Why? Well, for example, regardless of the fact that the exercise is set up so each team is directed to operate in the best interests of the overall organization, teams quickly get caught up in a competitive spirit and a desire to "win." In and of itself, of course, this can be very positive—it just has to be directed at the "right" target. External rather than internal competition.

The result in this case, however, is that teams are reluctant to share information. And they tend to view anyone requesting information—regardless of how logical and compelling the explanation for the request may be—with skepticism, even mistrust. Teams then tend to hunker down and play their cards even closer to their vests, further inhibiting the possibility of productive negotiations.

This issue of trust—or, perhaps more accurately, the lack thereof—also rears its ugly head during normal negotiations, even absent a "trigger" like a misinterpreted request for information. Just in general, teams wonder whether other teams are "telling the truth" about their needs, or whether they are exaggerating as a negotiating ploy. So they are reluctant to trade for fear of getting "hoodwinked."

3. **Communication.** Even when groups realize the importance of cooperating, they sometimes run into trouble because of simple communications. This tends to manifest itself in two ways: phraseology of questions and perspective of answers.

    For example, a seemingly simple question like, "How much (of a certain) resource do you need?" could trigger answers that range from total requirement to minimum acceptable requirement to the gap between actual and either total or minimum acceptable requirement. Without clarification, which almost never occurs, the result is that no real information has passed hands.

    In fact, in some ways it's worse than having not shared in the first place since now teams feel they have made some progress, that they now have some valid, usable information when, in fact, they may not. This feeling tends to be short-lived; however, as casual comments cause people to question the authenticity of earlier pronouncements regarding needs. This, in turn, tends to raise trust issues.

4. **Focus.** The initial reaction of virtually every team has been to go "heads down." To pull out the pencil and calculator and try to figure out what they

need to satisfy their own parochial objectives, and then to put a strategy in place to accomplish what they've decided on.

It is an understandable way of operating. A typical—or traditional—response. These are areas that people are comfortable with. Areas they have direct control over.

But this type of traditional response will not enable the teams to accomplish the overall objective. For that, the teams must work together because in this situation there are other parties involved—people from "multiple different" organizational units over whom the other teams do not have direct control. Anything that could potentially be accomplished has to be accomplished through influence rather than authority.

So the focus has to be transferred from internal to external, and from control to influence.

And with that shift in focus comes questions that may not have been asked with the previous mindset. For example, what are we really trying to accomplish here? What do we need to do from an overall perspective first, and then how can we make sure each of the individual units is "kept whole," or at least kept as whole as possible?

Certainly the teams need to understand their own situations. And ultimately, of course, they would have to "run the numbers," but only after those numbers had been placed within the context of the broader focus.

A simple framework to establish productive cross-functional relationships

Let's summarize. The four primary causes of dysfunctional cross-organizational relationships are assumptions, trust, communications and focus. Recognizing that allows us to develop specific suggestions regarding how to avoid pitfalls in these areas. We've developed a simple, straightforward framework—in the form of an acronym—that people have found useful in terms of establishing productive cross-functional relationships. The acronym itself, as most useful acronyms do, sends an overarching message. It is, S-H-A-A-R-E F-A-C-T-S. The implicit message, of course, is that when operating cross-functionally, people need to deal in data and facts, not with emotions, and not with personalities; and importantly, to be cognizant at all times of the Golden Rule of Leadership. We'll introduce a quick summary of each of these elements, and then we'll provide a full exposition of the framework.

Share information. And be willing to share first.

Help. Anyone you can, anytime you can, anyway you can.

Ask for help, if you need it.

Ask for clarification, if there is any potential for misunderstanding.

Relationships. Build them, nurture them.

Enjoy—find a way. Work is too big a part of our lives not to enjoy it.

Full disclosure. Over-communicate, if necessary, to avoid potential trust issues.

Assumptions. Surface and validate them.

Clear and precise language. Avoid misunderstandings and confusion.

Transfer focus. Look at the big picture first.

Show benefits. Have the evidence necessary to support your position.

Share information

This often means, "share information *first.*" Going to another person or group and asking them to "show you their hand," without first revealing yours, does nothing but engender mistrust. People naturally question your motivation and assume you are somehow trying to gain the upper hand. If you want someone else to share information with you, you must first be willing to share with him or her.

This is really nothing more than another application of the GRL. Think of how you would like to be treated. If someone came to you looking for information, wouldn't you like them to be willing to share?

Of course, the counterargument always is, "But I was going to share once they did." That may be true, but how would they know. They may legitimately fear that, once they shared their information, you might walk away without revealing anything. And if the request is put in the form of a "trade" (i.e., I'll share my information if you share yours), all that does is set the stage for a non-trusting relationship. Think about it. What it basically says is, "I don't trust you enough to share my information with you without a specific pledge on your part to reciprocate."

So, if you would like someone to share information with you, then you must be willing to take the risk of sharing with them—first.

Help

My personal philosophy is help anyone you can, anytime you can, anyway you can. Why? Well, one very human—and not unimportant—reason is that it feels good to help other people. But the more pragmatic organizational justification is that it's like putting money in the bank. The more people you help, the more people you can turn to when you run into trouble, as most people in organizations inevitably do.

We get an interesting reaction to this suggestion from groups with whom we work. Almost nobody disagrees with the philosophy. But lots of people just don't think it's practical—at least not in today's business environment. As the argument goes, everybody's too busy, too overworked, and too resource-constrained to help. If you spend resources—either your own time or that of people in your organization—you won't get your own job done. Lots of head nodding at that one.

And I can't argue with that. All those arguments are true. But counterarguments exist that I believe are even more persuasive. As an example, look at the Amish. They regularly hold "barn raising" parties, where virtually everyone in the community helps one of the members build a barn.

If they held the same parochial views as those expressed by some, a lot fewer barns would be built. One person simply cannot build a barn by him or herself. While the application is different, the concept is the same in the business world. Of course we're all too busy to help, but that is the very reason why we should help.

Ultimately, "the worm turns," as they say, and we will need help ourselves. If we haven't been willing to extend ourselves, there will be very few people standing in line waiting to help us when our turn comes.

Help, by the way, doesn't always mean sacrifice, although that is clearly sometimes the case. We can help in a number of ways without overstraining ourselves or our resources. For example, if we don't have the time or resources to provide direct assistance, we may be able to provide advice or tips on how to handle a specific situation. Even suggestions as to how we may have dealt with a similar "problem" might be helpful.

Or we may be able to refer the requestor to someone who may be able to help. Or to someone who knows someone who can help. Anyway, you get the idea. If at all possible, the answer should never be "no," no matter how nicely couched. "Sorry, I'd love to help, but we're out straight here as well…you understand…" is just "no" packaged with a prettier bow. Find some way to help.

Again, it's just the GRL. If you were in a situation where you needed help, wouldn't you want someone to step in and give you a hand? Of course you would, and so do others. So treat people the way you would like to be treated. Become the "go-to" person. It may seem like a strain at first, but in the end it makes you an invaluable member of the larger team. And, from a more pragmatic perspective, those types of efforts typically do not go unnoticed by more senior members of management.

Ask…for help

We're all too busy these days. No one is going to swing by your office, stick their head in the doorway, and say, "I don't have too much going on today. Is there anything I can do for you?" It's simply not going to happen.

If you need help, you have to ask for it. And that doesn't mean a "get on your knees" plea for assistance. It just means a simple request. "I've got a situation here, Charlie or Sally or whomever; just wondering if you've ever run into anything like this—whether you have any ideas…."

Charlie or Sally or whomever, if in business for any length of time, will understand you're looking for help. And, just to punctuate our previous point, what will be the first (even if implicit) thought that runs through their heads? "Have I ever asked this person for help, and, if so, what was his or her response?" If you've turned Charlie or Sally down before, don't expect a whole lot of sympathy now.

Case Example 1.

We did a lot of work with one client where, in almost every program, someone (usually more than one person) would say something like, "What we need is a company directory. That way, if we need help, we can simply find the right resource in the directory, call that person up, and get what we need."

Now that may sound like a naïve statement, and I suppose in many ways it is, but that's the way a lot of people in business think—and not just in this particular company. And there is some supporting logic. If the information in the directory is correct, and that's the person's job, then he or she should—perhaps even *must*—help.

But people are human. Let's assume that what you need falls exactly within the parameters of a job description you find in a corporate directory and you call this person—who you presumably have never met before (otherwise you wouldn't have needed the directory)—and ask for help.

Is that person sitting around with nothing to do? Obviously not. More than likely, just like you, that person has more to do—more requests from others like you in the organization—than the time or resources to do it. So who are they going to help? A faceless, nameless voice on the phone, or a known person who perhaps has helped them in the past. The answer is obvious.

With this particular client, when confronted with that statement about a corporate directory, we would often ask if there was anyone they knew who was somehow able to get things done even in the absence of such a directory. And in every group virtually everyone knew at least one such person. "Oh yeah," people would say. "Charlie (or Sally or whomever) always gets what he needs."

How is that, we would ask, since they don't have a directory either? "Oh, he or she just knows everybody" was the typical, and not unexpected, response. And how did they get to "know everybody?" Certainly not by just running around asking for help, I'm sure. Charlie or Sally sound like people who understand human nature—who understand that business is fundamentally a people game. If you begin to peel back the onion, I'm sure you would find that Charlie and Sally, over the years, had put a lot of "money in the bank" in terms of building relationships across the organization.

Case Example 2.

We had another client—an individual—a few years back, who was one of these Charlie/Sally types. Someone who just seemed to know everyone in the company. Who always seemed able to get things done—to get what she needed from almost anyone in the organization. And yet, she was relatively new to the company. In fact, her boss commented that she had gotten to know more people in the company in three months than he had in thirty-five years.

Curious, we simply asked how she did it. How did she create such a robust network in such a short period of time? Her answer was instructive. When she first started at the company, whenever she had a question—or a request—for someone, instead of picking up the phone and calling (which would have been the easiest and fastest way to go about it), she would go to that person's office, stick her head in the doorway and introduce herself. Almost invariably, the other person would invite her in, they'd chat for a few minutes—just getting to know each other—and then she'd ask the question, always in an easy, relaxed, non-threatening way, and always in a way that acknowledged that the other person probably had too much on their plate already, but if they could at least point her in the right direction....

Again, magic. By going to the office instead of phoning she was able to make face-to-face contact. By spending a few minutes building rapport, she was able to develop a personal connection. And by honoring the time of the other person, she disarmed the normal defense mechanisms of people who are short on time and who must jealously guard it.

But how about the other side of the coin—did she provide help when asked for it? Absolutely. In fact, she would often help even if she weren't directly asked, and not only for normal business requests. For example, this particular company hosted an annual charity event—kind of an outside fair—where company employees would play music, serve food, etc. One year it rained, and everyone ran inside leaving the hapless musician—one of the company's employees—in the unfortunate position of having to cart all his equipment—keyboard, amps, and so on—inside. The only person who stayed to help was this woman. She got just as soaked as the musician, and she didn't leave his side until every piece of equipment was safely indoors.

He never forgot that incident. Years later he would still relate that story to anyone who would listen, and he was always available to help this woman whenever she needed it.

So, for sure, ask for help when you need it. But make sure you plant the seeds before that day comes.

Be Upfront

The other side of asking for help is being upfront and honest. We all know people who try and ask for help in such a way as to suggest that what they're asking for is really a benefit to you, and, in effect, not a request for help at all. A few years back, I attended a conference. The speaker at a breakout session that I had joined just before lunch suggested that, as a favor to the group, he was going to wrap up early so people would be able to freshen up or make phone calls before lunch.

Well, it turns out that, not surprisingly, people had planned their day around the conference schedule. There had been a break just before his session, and there was ample time for "freshening up" and phone calls—as well as eating—during the luncheon intermission. There really was no legitimate reason to end the session early.

The group's reaction: the speaker's *offer* was a pretense—that he must have some other reason for ending early. They felt they had lost out on information they had come to the conference to obtain. (As a postscript, we later learned that this speaker had a luncheon appointment across town and wanted to get an early start so he'd be sure to be on time.)

The end result: a loss of credibility. While the group didn't know at the time exactly what his real reason for ending early was, his "favor" was perceived to be exactly what it was—an attempt to convince the class that they were receiving a favor instead of conferring one, which, in actual fact, was what was happening.

Again, the GRL. Treat people the way you would like to be treated. If someone came to you looking for a favor, you would want them to be upfront about it. You certainly wouldn't want them to try and "trick" you into thinking they were doing you a favor. Well, likewise, if you need a favor, say so. Don't try to couch it in language that suggests you're doing the favor for the other person. If there is a real benefit to the other party, by all means say so, but do it within the context of what the real request is.

Ask...for clarification

This one stands on its own. On important points, it's critically important you understand precisely what the other party is saying. Particularly when it comes to the numbers.

That is one of the biggest impediments to progress in simulated negotiations we hold. People tended to make assumptions about what other parties were saying. So, for example, if someone said they needed a certain amount of resource, did that mean that was their total requirement? Or was it the gap between the number they started with and their total requirement? Or was it the gap between the number they started with and what they needed to make a minimum acceptable target?

Rarely did anyone ever ask for clarification. Everyone went forward making his or her own assumptions about what the answer meant. You can imagine the havoc this caused as teams attempted to juggle resources around in order meet both their individual team bogies, and the overall objective. It was next to impossible for people to get a "fix" on where they were or what they needed to do as an enterprise, since most people were working with different numbers.

Plus, this lack of clarity tended to generate trust issues as seemingly conflicting statements were made by teams in response to differently phrased questions, or comments made to shore up arguments. Most groups went to the last round of negotiations not really knowing where they stood as a whole. And often they ended up making trades on faith in the last couple of minutes in the hopes of satisfying the objectives.

And yet, this confusion could easily have been averted by asking a few simple questions. Of course, the challenge in any situation like this is that people don't realize they've made an assumption, and, therefore, don't realize there is confusion. If they did, they would obviously ask the necessary questions to clear it up.

So how do people get to the point that they realize they're making an assumption rather than dealing with a fact? Very easy. They just have to train themselves to ask one simple question. "Is this an assumption or a fact?" If the answer is "assumption," then they realize they must ask one or more clarifying questions. If the answer is "fact," they can move confidently forward.

This doesn't mean the flow of every conversation must be constantly interrupted by that question. Some things are obviously facts, and some are obviously assumptions. It just means that where there is the possibility for confusion that question should be asked.

One example is numbers. Numbers are almost always fertile ground for misunderstandings and confusion. So anytime you're in a situation where you must deal with numbers, which is probably often for most of us, be alert to the need to ask if something is an assumption or a fact.

Another example is when people say things like, "You know what I mean..." or "enough said..." or other vague statements or unfinished sentences. Ask the person to clarify what they mean.

This can be done in a very non-threatening way. You don't have to say, for example, "Finish your sentence, will you...." Rather, you can gently say, "Could you please help me understand...?" Or, "I'm not sure I'm following you, could you say that another way?" This puts the burden of the misunderstanding on you, which allows the other person to save face, while at the same time putting them in a position where they must clarify what they've said.

Ultimately, the burden of understanding is on our shoulders. We're the "losers" if we move forward, basing our actions and decisions on incorrect assumptions. So it behooves us to make sure we have an accurate understanding of what the other person is saying.

This really is just another application of the Golden Rule. If someone misunderstood something you were saying, wouldn't you want that person to ask for clarification? To be sure that he or she understood the issue and your perspective on it. You certainly wouldn't want anyone to pass along an inadvertent misrepresentation of your position.

So treat other people the same way. If you're not sure, then ask for clarification. An experienced businessperson won't feel threatened by this, particularly if you ask in a discreet, non-threatening manner. In fact, an experienced businessperson will, more than likely, appreciate your interest and your questions. After all, if you have a misunderstanding, then perhaps others do as well, and it gives the person a chance to clear all that up.

Relationships

Business is a people game—we've noted this before, and we'll note it again. Business is all about relationships. The more relationships you can build across the organization (or even outside the organization, depending on your position), the better off you'll be. Almost nowhere is the GRL more applicable than when it comes to relationships. Keep it in mind as you read through this section.

So the question obviously is, how does one go about building relationships? The best guide is probably your own experience. Take what has been successful for you in the past and replicate it. Beyond that, there are a few simple things that we've found helpful in initiating relationships and building a solid foundation for maintaining them. To the degree that they make sense to you, you may want to give them a try. It gets down to three simple rules: building rapport, sharing and caring.

Building Rapport

Building rapport is not just for a first meeting. It's something that's done every time you get together with someone else, regardless of how well you know him or her, or regardless of how long you've had a relationship.

It's kind of the interpersonal equivalent of walking slowly into a cold ocean. Most of us who are past our teenage years don't just run wildly at the water and dive in. We wade slowly in, pausing occasionally to allow our bodies to adjust to the temperature, and then take a few more steps.

That's building rapport. Wade slowly into the discussion. Allow yourself, and the person you're talking with, time to adjust to the conversation. And then move on. So what topics do we use to build rapport? Regardless of what some people may tell you, weather is a good old standby. It's a quick opener. Everybody's comfortable with it.

Depending on who you're speaking with, sports may be a possibility. And traffic (or travel, depending on location and how you got there) is another. Or, if you're in the other person's office, comments or questions about pictures, decorations or mementos in the room can be a source of rapport building. You just need to tread a little lightly here to avoid the appearance of prying.

I was chatting recently with a client, a human resources professional, who was trying to help a manager—one of her internal "clients"—improve his interpersonal skills. They went together to a meeting at the office of a business partner of the manager—one of his internal customers with whom he had a strained relationship.

Sitting on the desk was a picture of a woman holding a newborn baby. After the normal, and very brief, "hello's," the HR professional waited, expecting the manager to make the obvious comment, "What a beautiful baby," or ask the obvious question, "Did your wife just have a baby?" or something to that effect.

Instead, the manager launched into a review of the business purpose of the meeting, which was to resolve some issues that had impeded progress in meeting their respective objectives. He laid out an agenda and moved on to the first topic.

All done very professionally. And his business partner responded very professionally. And, when the hour-long meeting was over, they had resolved nothing. In fact, in one sense they left the meeting in somewhat worse shape than they began because it was yet another failed attempt at coming to a meeting of the minds. Positions on both sides had hardened somewhat, and both parties went away, I'm sure, more convinced than ever of the intractability of the other person.

After the meeting the HR professional asked the manager if he had seen the picture. Yes, he assured her, he had seen it. She then asked why he hadn't commented on it. His response was he was there on business and didn't feel the picture had anything to do with business.

Was he right? Yes and no. "Yes" because, in some sort of formal sense, I suppose, the picture didn't have anything to do with the specific purpose of the meeting. "No" because a business meeting is, by definition, an interaction between people. And that means that "people things" are part of the meeting. Think GRL. Wouldn't you appreciate it if someone showed some interest—in a non-intrusive way, of course—in you personally? Wouldn't you, for example, have liked an opportunity to talk about your new baby? Most parents I know are just dying for the chance to do that. Wouldn't you have appreciated someone giving you that very opportunity?

So treat people the way you would like to be treated. Build rapport. Show some interest. Give the other person a chance to tell you a little about him or herself.

Back to the meeting. Would it have gone differently had the manager commented on the picture? Maybe, maybe not. But it was certainly worth a try. It might have helped the two parties establish some sort of personal "connection" that would have allowed them to more easily work through their differences.

It would have meant that the manager had to take a risk. The business partner could have rebuffed the manager's attempt to build rapport and moved directly into the purpose of the meeting. The manager may have been embarrassed or may have gone away with hurt feelings, and it may have further solidified the manager's belief that personal things have no place in business meetings.

And all that would have been very unfortunate. I must say, however, that in my experience it is very rare for someone not to respond to innocent attempts at rapport building. Most people intuitively understand the flow, the process, and they're as interested as you are in making it work.

For the most part, when it doesn't work, there's either some history of "bad blood" between the two parties, or one or both of the parties has come into the relationship with some preconceived notions about an adversarial relationship.

Sharing and Caring

Once rapport is established, the relationship building process is one of give and take, of sharing and caring. Just as we stated in our narrative of the first "S" in our S-H-A-A-R-E F-A-C-T-S acronym, when building a relationship, it's important that we be willing to share personal information, and that we be willing to share first. That doesn't mean that immediately after being introduced to someone we begin to "spill our guts." There would probably be no surer way to end the relationship before it got started.

Caring is simply being interested in the other individual as a person—caring about what they say, caring about them as a human being—in short, applying the Golden Rule. There's a flow in the process of building a relationship. Sharing and caring are iterative, recursive. First we share, and then we care. Then we share some more and care some more, and so on. Start slow with the sharing. It can be as simple as a comment about the forum in which you happen to be meeting. If at a conference, for example, you could say something like, "This is my third year here. I find these conferences helpful." More than likely that will encourage a similar comment from the person you've just met.

From there, you can begin to expand the sharing of information, probably focused on business at first, but ultimately getting into some light, non-threatening personal areas. At each step in the flow, you will find there are natural opportunities for each of you to share and care.

It is this process of sharing and caring that builds the relationship. It takes time and energy. It's an investment. And, like any investment, people naturally want to protect it, nurture it, and, ultimately, get a payback. The "payback," in a relationship sense, is really nothing more than a continual maturing of the relationship—the development of some sort of bond.

And the payback is manifested in a business sense as well. People—business partners—who have formed a personal relationship are much more likely to try harder to work through difficult issues and problems. To try and find solutions. To come to some accommodation. And this, of course, is particularly helpful when trying to work effectively across organizational boundaries.

Enjoy

We all work too hard these days. Spend too many hours at the office, and not enough time at home. If we don't enjoy what we do, or if we can't find some way to enjoy our work, it will have a dramatic effect on our quality of life.

While there may be a myriad of possibilities regarding why you don't enjoy what you do, basically they boil down to two reasons. Either you don't enjoy what you actually *do* (i.e., the particular functions of the job itself), or you don't enjoy the people you work with. Let's take the second one first.

Possibility One: You don't enjoy the people you work with

Again, your own experience here is the best guide. Take what you have found to be successful in dealing with people you don't enjoy working with, and apply it to other similar situations you may be facing.

In addition, here are a few suggestions we've found to be of help in injecting more "joy" into your working life. They basically involve changes in mindset, which are not easy. But the alternative is continuing to spend a significant percentage of your life being less than happy. This is a very important point! Your state of mind impacts your quality of life, your business day—and, perhaps, business decisions—in more ways than you might think.

1. **Accept people for who they are.** One of the biggest impediments to enjoying your job is working with difficult people. It has multiple negative effects. The first, and most obvious, is the actual encounter with the person. But there are after effects as well. There's the "upset" after an unpleasant experience that can linger, sometimes for hours. There's the "venting" that often occurs after the fact when you relate the incident to caring friends. There's the dreaded anticipation of the next encounter. And so on.

   So, how do you deal with this? One of the reasons the encounter tends to be so unpleasant is that we, as human beings, tend to "hope" it won't happen again. That something will have changed. That the unpleasant party will have undergone some sort of metamorphosis and will now act in a more civil fashion.

   In effect, what we've done is built a set of expectations about the other individual's behavior. And it's actually those unmet expectations, as much as it is the other person's behavior that causes the upset.

   The reality is that it's very unlikely the person will have somehow miraculously changed. In order to make the next encounter less personally taxing, the first thing we need to do is establish a set of realistic expectations for ourselves. Understand this is the way that person is, and expect him or her to behave in the same way the next time we deal with him or her.

   Does that mean that somehow it will now not bother us because we expect it? Not totally, but my guess is that it will bother you a lot less. If you expect it, you'll be more prepared for it, more ready and able to deal with it.

2. **Reframe the situation.** I'm not a psychologist, so please do your own research to validate (or invalidate) the following comments, but recent theories seem to suggest that "venting" may not work as well as advertised. Venting, as we all

know, is intended to release, or vent, the anger and upset, and allow us to get past it and move on. It turns out that what it actually does is cause us to relive the experience, which causes us to become angry and upset all over again. Which means we have to vent some more. Which means we get angry and upset again. And so on.

It's a vicious cycle. And the only one hurt is us. The person we're venting about doesn't even know we're venting. That person is going on about his or her business while we're continuing to get more and more angry and more and more upset. It's been said that being angry with someone is like drinking poison and expecting that other person to drop dead. The anger eats away at us—it doesn't do anything to the person we're angry at.

Reframing is the alternative to venting. Example: We've all probably had the experience of driving along in our cars and having someone race past us in a dangerous and reckless fashion—perhaps even to the point of coming close to endangering us. One common, human, response is to get angry. To swear. To complain to ourselves or the people riding with us about what a jerk the other driver was.

And that all may be true. But how does it help us? The reality is that it doesn't. It just causes us to be upset for a longer period of time. Reframing says you essentially develop a plausible alternative scenario to explain the other person's actions. So, in the case of the reckless driver, instead of assuming that he or she is simply a jerk, how about assuming that they are racing to the hospital with a sick spouse or child. If that scenario were true, we would probably be much more likely to feel sympathy for the other driver than anger.

But, the counterargument goes, how do we know they're driving someone to the hospital? We just made it up. True. But how do we know they're a jerk? We just made that up too. Any conclusions we draw about the driver's behavior are essentially made up and based solely on that one experience. And any of them could be true. So why not choose one that makes us less angry, less upset. The incident is over. Why not just allow ourselves to get past it quickly rather than reliving it, re-telling it, and potentially re-energizing the anger and upset.

Reframing can work anywhere, not just on the highway. But, like anything else, it's not necessarily instinctive—it's a learned habit. The more we practice it, the better we'll get at it. The first few times—or perhaps the first many times—we try it, it may not work. We may not even "buy" our own reframing. But ultimately we'll get the hang of it and it will start to pay dividends in terms of our perspective on unpleasant encounters and our ability to quickly get past them.

3. **Examine our own behavior.** I suppose it's possible, even if it isn't likely, that we are the ones who are inadvertently creating the unpleasant situation, perhaps without even realizing it. Do a quick mental check of past encounters. Is there anything you've said or done that could have caused the other person to act in a difficult manner? Is there anything you could do differently the next time around that might help avoid that type of situation?

4. **Build rapport, share and care.** In your own mind, start the relationship all over again. Try all the things we mentioned earlier. Begin each meeting with a little rapport-building. Share a light anecdote about yourself—from either a personal or business perspective. Express interest in the other person. Try to build a relationship.

   This may require you to set aside some of your own potentially negative feelings about the other person. Not an easy thing to do. But, as the old religious song says, "Keep your eyes on the prize."[6] Remember that your objective is to improve your quality of life by putting more enjoyment into your work-a-day world. Building a more comfortable working relationship will help you achieve that goal. Given the scenario we've laid out here, it doesn't look like the other person is going to extend him or herself to reach out to you, to do the types of "fence-mending" we're talking about here. So it's up to you.

5. **Talk to the other person about the relationship.** Some people suggest this is the place to start, but our experience has been that it may be preferable to tread lightly here. Again, let your experience be your guide.

   What you want is to see if there's some way to resolve the unpleasant aspects of a given encounter. In my experience, it's not particularly helpful to be too direct, to state something like, for example, "We don't seem to have gotten off to a very good start here, maybe we can start over...."

   What I've found is that people tend to "hunker down," feign ignorance, deny they're even aware of what you're talking about, and proclaim it's "just business," or words to that effect.

   This is not very helpful, and, in fact, potentially hurtful, since now the "gauntlet" has been thrown down, and the possibility of resolving the difficulties in a more indirect way has potentially been eliminated.

   On the other hand, some would say, what have you got to lose? If the situation is that bad, why not at least try to resolve it with the direct approach. I really can't find fault with that thinking, either.

   But perhaps the best suggestion is to hold this one out as a last resort. Try a more indirect approach first. Rather than addressing the relationship as "the problem," focus on the issue as the culprit. Readdress the objective. What is it you are mutually trying to accomplish? Try to find common ground—aspects of the situation you agree on. Reach agreement as to the areas where your positions are not in concert and see if you can put a plan in place to address those issues.

Then, if all that fails, lay the cards on the table. But even here I'd suggest approaching it gingerly, taking care not to point fingers. Perhaps even accept more of the responsibility than you actually feel. For example, "I hope I'm misreading this, but I'm sensing some discomfort on your part. Have I offended you in some way? If so, I'd like an opportunity to make amends."

6. **Grin and bear it.** If all else fails, just accept the fact that there are going to be some people you don't enjoy working with as an unpleasant fact of life. Like bad weather. Floods. Tornadoes. Hurricanes. Something that just happens that we have no control over and can't do anything about.

The reality is that sometimes people just behave in an unpleasant manner, and that sometimes there's nothing we can do about it

Possibility Two: You don't enjoy what you actually do

The other possibility is that you simply don't like what you actually do—the functions of the job itself. In many ways this may be almost as difficult to overcome as the "people" challenge we discussed above. And, as above, a large part of the answer, I suspect, has to do with how we view our situation.

Martha Washington said, "The greatest part of our happiness depends on our dispositions, not our circumstances." Hugh Downs[7] agreed when he said, "A happy person is not a person in a certain set of circumstances, but rather a person with a certain set of attitudes." But, perhaps most pertinent to the topic under discussion was Wilfred A. Peterson's[8] point. "Happiness doesn't come from doing what we like to do," he said, "but from liking what we have to do."

Of course, it's easier to agree with the sentiments in a few short quotes than it is to follow their dictates. What follows are a few thoughts on happiness (read that as "enjoyment") that may help in our situations.

As we all know, this issue of employees not liking their jobs is not uncommon. In fact, that's exactly the situation the automobile industry finds itself in. For more than a hundred years, study after study has shown that assembly line workers in automobile plants hate their jobs. They find them "mind-numbing," and often have to "think about something else" just to get through the day.

That's true for virtually every automobile company—except Toyota. At Toyota assembly line workers love their jobs. Why? On the surface it's the same exact job. So what creates this vast difference in the perspective of the workers?

I had the opportunity to spend some time at Toyota, and had a chance to talk with assembly line workers. When asked why they loved their jobs, the answer was the same. It had nothing to do with money (and Toyota workers are well paid, but that's true in virtually all automobile companies). It had nothing to do with working conditions (although Toyota's plants are spotlessly clean and well-maintained). It actually had nothing to do with the job itself, which, on the surface at least, was essentially the same as similar jobs in virtually every automobile company.

No, the answer was both much simpler and much more complex than any of those possible explanations. "I love my job," Toyota workers would say, "because for the first time in my career somebody actually listens to what I have to say, and by gosh, they do what I suggest."

Pretty profound. And there's an important message for us there, both from an "enjoyment" perspective, and from a "leadership" perspective. We'll address the latter in the next chapter, but for now let's focus on enjoyment.

When Toyota workers talk about people listening to them and doing what they suggest, what they're really saying is that Toyota gives them the opportunity to make suggestions about how to improve their jobs. And that, in effect, gives them some control over what they do and how they do it. And that's what makes them enjoy their jobs.

Enjoyment and happiness may not technically be exactly the same, but for purposes of our discussion here, let's equate them. An excellent study done a few years ago by ABC News[9] attempted to determine the factors that contributed to happiness. Academicians, researchers, and numerous psychologists, along with other professionals, were consulted. A wide and varied cross section of people was interviewed. Case studies were developed. And when all was said and done, the results identified six factors as leading to happiness: control, optimism, belief in God, activity, relationships and purpose.[10] One particular group, the Amish, was cited as being particularly happy.[11]

Case Analysis: The Amish

It sounds implausible, doesn't it? This is the group that denies modern conveniences: electricity, automobiles, lawnmowers, and so on. Things most of us now consider necessities, not luxuries.

Many, if not most, people would think this is a very difficult way to live. That you would, out of necessity, be so caught up in the "daily grind" of eking out an existence, that you wouldn't have time to be happy.

So how could that be? Well, let's go back to the list of happiness factors. Clearly the Amish are in control of their lives. They must rely on themselves in order to live. There's no welfare. No food stamps. No governmental "safety net" to access. They do it all themselves.

Because they are in control, and because they have a long history of successfully dealing with the events that can impact their lives, they are very optimistic about the future and their ability to deal with whatever they may encounter.

God, of course, is an integral part of their community, and their faith helps to form a solid foundation for their earthly existence. And they are constantly engaged in meaningful activities. Activities that many of us, perhaps, might think of as unnecessary. Why? For example, would you grow vegetables when you could just go to the supermarket? Yet these activities themselves are a critical element of their happiness.

Relationships are also an integral part of their community existence. Individuals don't attempt to build a barn by themselves, for example. The entire community assists in "barn raising," an event that is part social and part work. This shared effort, where each individual essentially helps every other individual, is a major contributor to the building, maintaining and strengthening of relationships.

And purpose. The entire lives of the Amish are built around purpose. Living lives in accordance with their belief in God. Providing for and caring for themselves and each other. Raising children. Building the community. Everything they do has a purpose that is important and meaningful to them.

So does this mean we all must sacrifice our worldly conveniences and become like the Amish? Well, in a way, yes. And, in another way, no. We certainly don't have to give up the types of modern conveniences we now take for granted.

But we probably should become more like the Amish in terms of their focus on those six factors we've discussed. (Or at least five of the six. If your particular belief system does not include a deity, perhaps you could substitute your own personal value system for that factor.)

Happiness and the Golden Rule

And, perhaps more to our overall point, we probably should emulate the Amish in terms of their adherence to the Golden Rule. Take another look at the six keys to happiness in relation to the Amish and the Golden Rule. Treating people like we would like to be treated is essential at every point. If we, for example, want control in our lives, then shouldn't we treat other people that way? Shouldn't we give them some control?

The same with optimism. If that's a key to our happiness, then the same is true for others. We need to help them see the future—that is, the realization of the vision—as a positive, work-enriching place to be. And I suppose a belief in God, in one sense, could be construed as a belief in adherence to the Golden Rule, since that "rule" is integral to so many religions.

And, just as our engaging in meaningful activities leads to our happiness, so would it lead to happiness for others. So do what we can to give people the opportunity to be so engaged. Relationships, of course, as we have seen, are all about the Golden Rule. And purpose, in many ways, could be thought of as a substitute for vision, with all the GRL implications we discussed above.

So, back to the point we started with in this part of our discussion. If we don't enjoy what we do—i.e., the functions of the job itself—what do we do? Of course, one easy answer might be to simply get a different job. But who's to say we'd like that any more than we did the other one.

No, before going that route, you may want to at least apply the principles of happiness we've just discussed. Find a way to establish more control over what you do and how you do it. Take a more optimistic view of your circumstances. (By the way, optimism—in the context within which we're referring—is a function of a positive attitude and self-confidence. Self-confidence, in turn, is a function of believing that you have the knowledge and skills necessary to successfully do your job. If that's not true in your situation, you may find that getting some additional training or coaching—if only from a colleague—may do wonders for how you view your job and your situation.)

Focus more on your God or your values than yourself. Think about what you have rather than what you don't have. Throw yourself into your work. Get so engaged that you simply don't have the time to think about how much you don't like what you're doing. Resolve to be the best you can possibly be at what you do.

Most important, focus on your relationships with the people around you at work. Follow the basics we referred to earlier. Build rapport, share and care. And, finally, find a purpose in what you're doing. Maybe that purpose is not directly related to your job. For example, you may have an outside activity you really enjoy, but couldn't do if you didn't have the income from your job. So the job then becomes an enabler of accomplishing your purpose.

Full Disclosure

As we have stated, one of the greatest impediments to successfully working with others, particularly (in an organizational sense) across functional boundaries, is a lack of trust. So we must do everything possible to prevent that from becoming an issue.

That means when it comes to sharing information, we would be better off *over*-sharing than *under*-sharing. For example, it would be quite natural to hold back information we believe to be irrelevant to the particular issue we're dealing with. Yet, if the other party senses we're "playing our cards too close to our vest," and not sharing information, the issue of trust may become a factor. Remember, if they don't know what the information is that we're holding back, they can't possibly know it's irrelevant.

Really, very little in an organization can't be shared across boundaries. After all, we all work for the same company. We all have the same overarching mission. Yet, for the most part, most of us (quite naturally, I believe) tend to treat our particular functional information as being somehow privileged. Departmental or divisional "secrecy" is fairly deeply engrained in many organizations.

I will grant you that there are instances where functional units within an organization cannot share information. But those instances, I believe, are relatively rare, and usually exist in industries that are regulated, or in companies that have some regulated divisions, and some unregulated divisions.

At a minimum, if you find yourself unwilling to share, at least examine why. You may find that you come to the conclusion that your concerns are not warranted. But if you are still unwilling to share, then at least remove the trust issue by explaining your rationale to the person(s) with whom you are dealing. Better they know you're holding back—rather than just suspect it—and better they know why. Again, employ the GRL. If you were in their position, wouldn't you want to be given that courtesy? So give it to them. They may not agree with your reasoning, but at least you will have been open about what your concerns are, which may help to alleviate any trust issues that could have developed.

Full disclosure, even disclosure as to why you are not able to disclose, is necessary to building trust. But it's not sufficient. As we stated earlier, trust is a function of five things: authenticity, credibility, relationships, and personal and business risk. Remember the equation we introduced:

$$\text{Trust} = \frac{\underline{\text{Authenticity} \times \text{Credibility} \times \text{Relationship}}}{\text{Risk}^2}$$

Let me give you an example. Let's suppose a friend of yours comes up to you and asks to borrow $10. He says that if you loan him the money, he'll pay you back $15 next week.

Is the person authentic? Is he who he seems to be? Is he honest and forthright? Let's assume the answers to all of the above are, "yes."

How about credibility? Let's assume you've known him for a long time, and his word has always been good. He has a history of saying what he means, and doing what he says. He performs, and he performs reliably in similar situations. You've loaned him money before, and he's always paid it back.

What about the relationship? Well, for purposes of our little example, let's assume he's a good friend and has been so for a long time. You know him well. You and he have shared personal information. There is a bond.

Okay, that leaves risk. In this example, we're really referring only to personal risk, since this isn't a business transaction. But I think the extension into business is pretty straightforward.

What's the harm if he doesn't pay you back the $10, let alone the $15 that he has promised? Well, nobody wants to be out $10 or $15, or, perhaps more importantly, no one wants to be "used," to be tricked into giving up money on the basis of false promises of repayment. But, let's face it; most of us would not be hurt very much if the money were not repaid in full, or even if it were not repaid at all. The fact is, many people wouldn't even notice. There is very little risk.

So we go ahead and loan him the $10. Sure enough a week later he comes back and gives us $15. All well and good.

Now, let's suppose that same individual comes back a couple months later and tells you that he's just gotten off the phone with his broker. His broker has given him a "hot tip," a stock that's expected to double in two months. So he asks you if he can borrow $25,000, and he promises to pay back $37,500 in two months. Should you trust him?

Well, let's see. Is the person authentic? Sure, nothing's changed there, as far as we know.

Does he have credibility? Again, sure. If anything, more than before, because the last time he promised to pay you a fifty percent return on your "investment" in only one week. And he made good on his word.

How about the relationship? Yes, again. Nothing has changed. He's still a good friend.

But what about risk. It's one thing to risk losing $10 or $15, it's quite another to risk losing $25,000. Risk has increased dramatically. And as risk has increased, trust has decreased.

Should you lend him the money? Your call. But I wouldn't. Too risky for my blood.

So, if you want to increase trust, do whatever you can to be authentic, to enhance credibility. Work on the relationship. And, in any possible interaction, do whatever you can to minimize risk—both personal and business.

Assumptions

We mentioned this a fair amount before. In business, we have to operate on assumptions. We do it every day. In fact, it's rare we would have all the facts regarding any given situation that we may face.

But, for the most part, we recognize, either implicitly or explicitly, that we are basing our actions and decisions on assumptions. The danger comes when we inadvertently work with an assumption and treat it as a fact.

We saw that in our exercise (described above). People would make all sorts of assumptions and treat them as facts. Assumptions about the conditions of other teams. Assumptions about the scoring structure. Assumptions about motivation.

For the most part, participants on these teams didn't question these assumptions. And that's where the mistake was made. It wasn't in the act of making assumptions. That's standard business practice—we couldn't stay in business if we didn't make assumptions. It was in the lack of realization that they were, in reality, assumptions.

So the real message here is not to forgo making assumptions, but rather to surface and validate the assumptions we have made. This is particularly important when faced with new or unusual situations. Faced with challenges that we deal with on a regular basis, we probably intuitively distinguish between facts and assumptions, just based on past experiences.

But in new situations, we may not have the necessary background and experience to make those implicit determinations. In those cases, it's critically important we just ask one simple question: Is this an assumption, or is this a fact? If the answer is you're not sure or that you believe it to be an assumption, then the obvious course of action is to validate it.

I've heard some people say they can't afford the time to ask that question. My response is that you probably can't afford not to. And it really doesn't take a lot of time. The question itself, when verbalized, probably consumes less than a second or two. Not a huge investment of time. And yet it can pay enormous dividends if it causes you to realize you've been treating one or more assumptions as facts.

Clear and Precise

Language can be tricky. Words can be misconstrued. As a result, intent can be misconstrued. Trust issues can arise. Relationships can be lost. Deals can be broken. All because someone used unclear and imprecise language.

Granted someone could do that deliberately, although I believe that's the exception, not the rule. More likely, someone innocently makes a statement that someone else may misunderstand and, therefore, inadvertently take inappropriate action.

Again, we saw this all the time in our exercise. People stating their needs honestly and forthrightly, but using imprecise or unclear language.

Other people accepting the statements and moving forward. Not realizing that what they heard was not what was said—or, perhaps more precisely—not what was intended to be said.

When the mistake is discovered, it is often ascribed not to error, but to intent. Particularly if the resultant action accrues to the benefit of the person or team making the unclear statement.

The message is simple. Use clear and precise language. Since you're making the statement anyhow, you may as well make it understandable. It's just the Golden Rule. How would you like to be treated? Wouldn't you want the other party to use clear and precise language? Wouldn't you want the intent to be unambiguous? So treat others the same way.

Transfer Focus

Basically, people in organizations face two types of challenges. Those where they have direct control and those where they do not have direct control—that require the use of influence rather than authority. The former are those challenges that fall totally within our specific area of responsibility. Technical problems, recalcitrant employees, obstinate customers, uncooperative suppliers—whatever it happens to be, it's something that's become a part of our daily work lives.

The latter challenges—let's call them "influence challenges," on the other hand, are those challenges that we face perhaps only occasionally. And when we face them, they tend to be different each time because they tend to involve different organizational units and, therefore, different people, some—or perhaps many—of whom we may have never dealt with before.

In these situations, we cannot simply mandate a solution. We must dig deeper. Do things we don't normally do. Change our focus. Understand a broader array of perspectives. Assimilate a more complex picture. All necessary if we're going to deal successfully with people we don't normally deal with, and if we're going to be able to accomplish what we need to accomplish.

That means we need to be explicitly conscious of—and practice—the GRL. This is not to suggest that the GRL is not equally important in dealing with challenges over which we do have control. It is. Rather, what we're suggesting is that, because this is a new, and potentially confusing, situation, it may be easy to inadvertently overlook the GRL.

In our exercise, for example, as we noted earlier, the first thing virtually every team does is go "heads-down." They pull out the paper and pencils and calculators and "run the numbers," and try to figure out what their own team needs to do to maximize their individual score.

They are comfortable with these things. These are things they do all the time. They have control over them. And if they had the authority—the direct control—over the other groups, they could just instruct the resources be redeployed in a certain way, and the exercise would be over in about fifteen minutes.

But the challenge is that they don't have that authority. They can't just "demand" that the resources be reallocated in a certain way. They must rely on the cooperation and support of other people who are outside their span of control. They must use influence rather than authority and that means they have to employ the GRL.

So how do you handle a specific situation that requires you use influence rather than authority? What we've found is people who are most successful in doing that execute a relatively straightforward five-step process:

1. The first thing they do is take a step back and shift their focus. They recognize they cannot resolve the problem in a vacuum. Therefore, they recognize they must, at a minimum, understand the overall challenge facing not only themselves, but also all the other parties who are involved as well. And they pay particular attention to—and are particularly sensitive to—the issues facing those other parties.

2. They recognize they don't have at their disposal all the information they need. So they must somehow gather that information. That means they must get the rest of the information from the other parties so they can piece together the entire puzzle. And that, in turn, means they must establish lines of communication.

    That means doing all the things we've stated in terms of building and nurturing relationships, sharing information first, validating assumptions, and so on. In other words, they treat people the way they, themselves like to be treated.

3. Once the lines of communication have been established, they work with the other parties to develop a process for arriving at a solution. Of course that process would vary depending upon the nature of the particular special challenge someone might face. But there are some common elements.

    For example, they do their homework. They make sure they understand where they, and each of the other parties, stand. And, within the context of the specific issue they're dealing with, they share what their objectives are, and how they are measured. And they work to learn and understand the other parties' objectives and measurement systems.

4. They protect each other. Again, in essence, they apply the Golden Rule. When and if it becomes clear that one or more parties would be hurt by whatever the plan happens to be, they "go back to the drawing board" to try and develop a different "scheme" that would meet the overall objectives while avoiding—to the degree possible—penalizing individual parties.

5. They execute the plan. This may seem like an obvious final step, but it's one that must not be overlooked. The people who are best at exercising influence understand that ultimately plans must be translated into action.

So how does all this relate to "our" issue—when faced with an "influence" challenge—of ensuring that we're appropriately shifting our focus? I think these are exactly the steps that must be taken. And it's important to pay particular attention to the fourth step, protect each other. (If someone feels he or she is going to be hurt by whatever resolution you come up with, they're going to resist it. It's not only human nature, it's organizational self-preservation.)

So, not surprisingly, we're back to the GRL. If you were one of the people who could be potentially hurt by the ultimate resolution of the challenge, how would you like to be treated? Even with the purest of motives, even with the best interests of the overall organization in mind, more than likely you would at least like to know your interests were protected. That people were doing everything they could to ensure you wouldn't be hurt.

Show Benefits

Sometimes, no matter how hard you try, no matter how logical your recommended solution, some people are just "not on board." In those situations, it's important to be ready to explain—in detail—how the proposed solution would benefit that person or that team.

In effect, that means preparing a "mini" business case. In our exercise, this often happened. The most well-off teams were often reluctant to give up their resources. Other teams then had to demonstrate why it would be of benefit to them.

And, again, this is really nothing more than the application of the GRL. If you were about to take an action (or not take an action) that could potentially prevent a group—of which you were a part—from achieving its objectives, wouldn't you want this pointed out to you? Wouldn't you want to have the opportunity to rethink your position and correct a potential mistake? So treat other people the same way you would like to be treated.

So there you have it: S-H-A-A-R-E F-A-C-T-S. It's a handy checklist when thinking about things you need to do if you have to work through other people outside your span of control. It's all about personal influence rather than authority. And it's all about acknowledging and implementing the Golden Rule of Leadership.

Step 5: Engage the Stakeholders—Key Points Summary

A. There are four primary causes of dysfunctional cross-organizational relationships:

1. Failing to validate assumptions

2. Mistrust

3. Breakdown in communication

4. Incorrect focus

B. There is a simple, straightforward way to overcome the causes of dysfunctional relationships, and to keep in mind the key leverage points in building effective cross-functional relationships:

Share—information, and be prepared to share first.

Help—anyone you can, anytime you can, anyway you can.

Ask—for help, if you need it.

Ask—for clarification, to ensure understanding.

Relationships—build them, nurture them.

Enjoy—find a way.

Full disclosure—when in doubt, share.

Assumptions—surface them, validate them.

Clear and precise language—use it to avoid misunderstandings, which can lead to mistrust.

Transfer focus—look at the big picture first.

Show benefits—help others see the big picture.

Pathway to Success
The Golden Rule and the
Leadership Process

Step 6: Energize the People

*Motivation is everything. You can do the work of two people,
but you can't be two people. Instead, you have to inspire the next guy down
the line and get him to inspire his people.*

Lee Iacocca

These days it's difficult to find anyone who doesn't know the "right words" to say when it comes to the issue of employee empowerment or employee engagement or other similar terms. Everybody *says* the right thing, but we've found very few companies—and very few leaders in those companies—who are actually *doing* the right things.

In this chapter we want to emphasize why it's important to engage employees in a fundamentally different way from what we've done in the past, and what the potential positive impact on your organization can be. And then we will explain ways that you can actually translate that critical concept into action.

Before we begin to do that, however, one quick comment. The focus of this chapter—Engage the People—is, in effect, the embodiment of the Golden Rule of Leadership. Engaging people is all about treating them the way you would like to be treated. Respecting their abilities. Listening to them. Honoring their ideas and suggestions. Appreciating their efforts and contributions. Saying and doing the things that you would like said and done if you were in their position.

So, at almost every turn in this narration, we could conceivably invoke the GRL. That, however, I believe, would be a continual restatement of the obvious. It would detract from the examples, and distract the reader from fully engaging in the flow of the narration.

Therefore, we have chosen not to do that, but rather to periodically remind the reader of the GRL by referencing it at points that we believe appropriate and useful to the general narration.

With that in mind, then, one straightforward formula to use when thinking about business performance in general is illustrated in the following framework:[12]

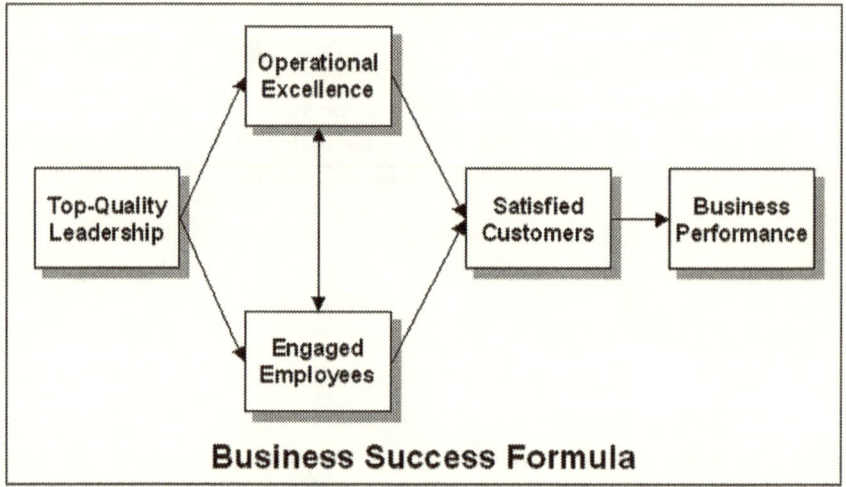

Business Success Formula

This formula is intended to be read from right to left. So basically what it says is if you want excellent business performance, you've got to have satisfied customers. No surprises there—everybody basically accepts that.

In order to have satisfied customers, you need to have operational excellence and engaged employees. Read operational excellence as quality products and services and quality processes, particularly those that "touch" the customer. Again, no surprises there. The Japanese have taught the world that quality is the key to satisfying customers.

The second input to satisfied customers, engaged employees, however, has been an area of controversy for a long time. Today, some companies still believe it doesn't matter. That if you hire people, pay them a decent wage, train them in terms of what they have to do and how they have to do it, and then make sure they do it, that it doesn't matter whether they're "engaged" or not. Kind of the old military model of the organization. We'll come back to this issue of engaged employees in a moment, since it is the core subject of this chapter.

The final element, top-quality leadership, is required in order to have operational excellence and engaged employees. Again, no magic here. Just about everyone agrees.

So let's come back to this issue of engaged employees. The sad fact is that until recently there was no empirical evidence to suggest that those "structural" organizations were wrong. Companies that did focus on engaging employees did so based on either anecdotal evidence or on faith alone. That is, they just simply believed that having truly engaged employees would lead to greater customer satisfaction.

Case Study: Sears

I say "until recently" because a few years ago Sears engaged in a comprehensive and intensive effort to develop a business model built around customers, results and employees. In 1992 Sears lost $3.9 billion—the worst year in its history. After a dramatic turnaround, which was largely the result of a change in strategy, the senior management of the company launched a campaign to revitalize the company by making it a "compelling place to shop." The results of their efforts were widely reported in the business press, most notably in an article in *Harvard Business Review*.[13]

After conducting numerous customer and employee surveys and focus groups, Sears developed the following formula to link employees, customers and business results:[14]

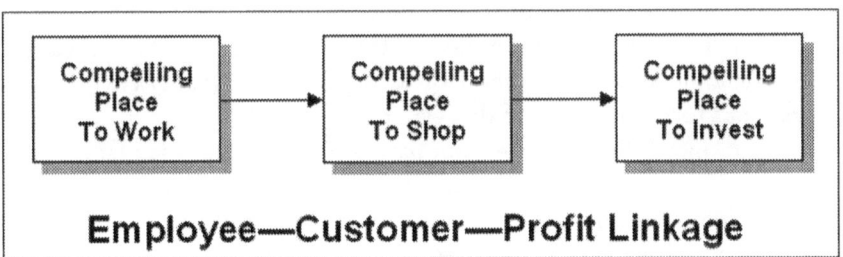

This formula, too, is read from right to left. If Sears is to be a compelling place to invest, then it must be a compelling place to shop (it's the customers who generate the revenues and profits that make it a compelling place to invest). And, if Sears is to be a compelling place to shop, it must be a compelling place to work (it's the employees who keep the customers coming back).

The idea was to develop a business model that would allow them to identify "cause and effect" relationships between the three elements and to develop frameworks and methodologies that would allow them to better manage the business. The result was what Sears calls their Total Performance Indicators (TPI).

While Sears feels the model has widespread applications across the business, in terms of the focus of this narrative the key finding is the direct linkage between "engaged" employees, satisfied customers, and business results. Sears found that a five-point increase in employee attitudes would result in a 1.3-point increase in customer satisfaction, which translates into a 0.5 percent increase in sales.

That 0.5 percent increase, however, was an absolute increase, not a percentage increase. So, in other words, if a comparison group of stores had an average "same store sales" increase of five percent, then the store with the improvement in employee attitudes would have an increase of 5.5 percent, not 5.025 percent. Sears, and I suspect most other retailers would agree, considered that a very significant impact.

So for the first time, there was empirical evidence that focusing on employees, truly engaging them, would have a positive impact on satisfied customers and business performance. This shouldn't come as a surprise to us at this point. In effect, it's nothing more than the Golden Rule. What Sears found is that if you treat people the way you would like to be treated, they respond.

So the real questions are: How do you engage employees? What does that mean? How do you know if they're engaged or not?

Input vs. Involvement

To begin to sort out the answers to these and other questions, let's return to Toyota. Toyota, as we noted earlier, is unique among companies in the automobile industry in that employees on the line truly love their jobs. Employees consistently recommend Toyota to their family, friends and neighbors as a great place to work, and Toyota has one of the—if not *the*—lowest turnover rates in the industry, and one of the highest—if not *the* highest—"perfect attendance" rates.

So what is it about Toyota that employees like so much? Remember what the employees themselves told us: "For the first time in my career somebody actually listens to what I have to say, and by gosh, they do what I suggest." Two very important messages are packed into that simple and touching statement.

First, people want to be listened to. They want to be respected. They want to be treated like people, and not like the traditional "cogs on a wheel."

Second, they want what they say to have some meaning. They're not just looking for "management" to listen sincerely with a grave countenance, nod in a fatherly or motherly fashion, and then walk away and act as if nothing had been said. They want people to take their suggestions seriously and to act on them. The issue isn't "input," it's "involvement."

Implementation Challenges

Companies—and managers—who have sincerely tried to implement "employee engagement" programs have run into a number of problems. And we've found that those problems oftentimes have derailed their efforts, causing them to fall back to some less comprehensive and/or intensive effort.

The problems tend to fall into three major areas:

❖ First, companies have found that the administrative task of analyzing and evaluating the volume of suggestions they get when they initiate some sort of employee engagement program is staggering. They simply don't have the time, people or money to handle the volume of suggestions they get.

❖ Second, they "argue" that employees typically don't have a broad enough perspective to make useful and meaningful suggestions. That the suggestions are simply not realistic.

❖ And third, their experience has been that even when employee suggestions have been realistic, they haven't been "implementable." Why? Because they've found that the time and cost of creating a new "standard" that incorporates the suggestion far exceeds the benefit they get from that suggestion.

So what is different about Toyota? Why haven't they experienced these types of problems, or, if they have, how have they been able to overcome them? How are they able to engage employees in such a dramatic fashion?

First some statistics, then we'll get to the answers to those questions. Think about this for a moment before you read on. How many suggestions do you think the average "Western" (i.e., American or European) worker makes in the course of a year?

Got an answer in mind? Okay, studies of companies that have formal employee suggestion systems have shown that the average Western worker makes about one suggestion every eight years.[15] That's staggering, isn't it? Far fewer than most people would imagine.

What about Toyota? How many suggestions does the average Toyota worker make? The answer: forty-one suggestions every year.[16] Just to be sure there is no misunderstanding—that's forty-one suggestions per employee per year. Staggering!

Of course, the real question is, how many of those suggestions are actually implemented? In western companies, the implementation is a very respectable thirty-two percent.[17] And at Toyota? Ninety-six percent![18]

If you do the math, that means that the average Toyota worker makes more than 325 times more suggestions than his or her "Western" counterpart. And more than 980 times more "implementable" suggestions. Toyota figures they benefit to the tune of about a half-billion dollars a year in savings just from employee suggestions. That's why the 2002 Corolla—more luxurious, with better quality and better features—cost Toyota less, and had a lower sticker price, than its 1997 predecessor. The only other industry where you see that happening is with computers, and that's a function of the technology.

Implementation Solutions

So how does Toyota do it, and how do they deal with the "problems" that other companies have encountered?

Well, first, Toyota has what I would call a "principles-based" employee engagement system, as opposed to the "process-based" systems we see in most other companies (more about this later). Their entire system is built around three key principles:

1. Team leaders (more on this, also, in a moment) must have a predisposition to say "yes."

2. Employees must focus on their own jobs when they make suggestions.

3. Unnecessary standards should not be imposed.

The reality is that in most companies we see, there is a predisposition on the part of management to say "no." That's true for some very practical reasons that get back to the "problems" these companies have experienced in trying to implement employee engagement systems. As we mentioned earlier, these companies have found that most suggestions are either not realistic or not implementable, and it takes an enormous amount of time to analyze and evaluate them. Since managers are already overworked, the last thing they want to do is spend a lot of time and energy analyzing something their experience (backed up by statistics) says will not be "doable" anyway.

So, much like an initial screening of resumes for a job posting (where "reviewers" first look for disqualifiers to make it easier to get through the pile), managers tend to keep a sharp ear tuned for reasons why they will be unable to approve employee suggestions.

The result of this, of course, is that employees quickly get disillusioned, discouraged, maybe even disgusted, and stop making suggestions. And the cold reality is that managers are often relieved when that happens, even if it isn't in "synch" with the party line.

Call Center Implementation Case Study

I worked with a company that, to its credit, was interested in getting employees engaged. It was a company that was in the "call center" business. The centers handled in-bound customer calls for new orders as well as repairs and maintenance. The company was operating on faith, believing that having engaged employees would lead to greater customer satisfaction.

Most call centers are highly structured, and this company's centers were no different. Associates literally read scripts off computer screens when handling customer calls, and calls were randomly monitored to ensure that associates were following the scripts. The only operation I can think of that might be more structured is an automobile assembly line.

In thinking about their desire to implement a system to "engage employees," the company decided to do a pilot first and then, if successful, implement the system in the same call center, and then go company-wide.

There were forty teams (of about twenty associates each) in the call center they selected for the pilot, and every team (and every associate) was evaluated monthly based on customer satisfaction ratings determined by follow-up calls to customers. Team rankings were posted monthly.

The team they selected turned out to be a marvelous group of energetic, highly motivated employees. But—and I think they would agree—they didn't start out that way. I confess that it isn't the team I would have selected for the pilot. Historically, month after month, this team had literally come in dead last—number forty—on the customer satisfaction ratings. At the conclusion of the pilot, one of the team members commented—only half in jest, I suspect—that in the past, if the team had risen to number thirty-nine in any given month, they would have had a meeting to find out what they had done *right* so they could correct it and get back to number forty the next month.

I still recall the very first meeting I had with the team as though it had happened yesterday. The bullets were flying fast and furious. Disbelief, disillusionment, cynicism and sarcasm were the order of the day. When I left I told the head of the call center that I didn't feel as though I was "leaving," I felt as though I was "escaping."

When I first mentioned the word "suggestion," somebody in the group said, "Oh yeah, the black hole." When I asked what they were talking about, they explained that every few years the company "launched" yet another "employee engagement" program and solicited suggestions. Typically they'd get a flood—a veritable tidal wave—of ideas. Far more than they could handle. Not only could they not implement them, they couldn't even evaluate them, so, for the most part, employees never even heard back on what the company had decided to do with their suggestions. Hence, the "black hole"—that's where their suggestions went.

Amazingly, we were able to work through their disillusionment and they agreed to give it yet one more try. We basically followed the tenets of Toyota's successful "principles-based" system; a predisposition to say "yes," focus on your own job, and don't impose unnecessary standards.

I must say this team—this group who had, in the past, consistently under-achieved—did themselves proud. Within two months they had actually risen to number one in the center. Number One. From fortieth to first place in two months, after years of languishing at the bottom of the customer satisfaction ratings.

The Hawthorne Effect

And they stayed there. I kept in touch for a time after my formal involvement ended, and they had remained at the top. So it wasn't a fluke. It wasn't a modern example of the Hawthorne Effect.

As a reminder of this now dated, but still relevant story; back in the mid-1920s General Electric funded a study at Western Electric's Hawthorne Works in Cicero, Illinois, to determine the effect of lighting on worker productivity. The anticipated finding was that brighter lighting would increase productivity and General Electric planned to use this hoped-for result in marketing its light bulbs.

Unfortunately (at least for General Electric's marketing plans), what they found was that almost any environmental change (including *decreasing* the lighting) resulted in improved productivity. After studying the situation, General Electric came to the ultimate conclusion that "lighting," per se, was irrelevant. The issue wasn't "wattage," it was "change." Employees tended to respond positively to any change—positive or negative—in their environment.

So the longevity of this call center team at the top proved—at least to my satisfaction—that this was not simply some sort of environmental effect. Rather, there was a fundamental change going on.

How they did it

And there were some humorous sidelights. The most telling was the behavior of the team who had typically occupied the top spot in terms of customer satisfaction. Associates on that team were literally crawling around on the floor trying to eavesdrop on the new "Number One's" to see what they were doing differently—what had catapulted them to the top.

We, of course, wanted to know that too. They had done a number of things, but one of the most interesting was how they chose to close each call with a customer. Remember that customer satisfaction was determined by follow-up calls to customers. They were asked to rate the service they had received on a sliding scale from "poor" to "outstanding," and there were three gradations in between.

This team decided to close each call by saying, in effect, "You may be receiving a call asking about the service you received today. I hope you feel it was outstanding." That did two things. First, it planted the word "outstanding" in the customer's mind. The team's thinking was that with that word firmly implanted, the customer would be more likely to rate the service outstanding. And they were right.

But the second, and equally important thing it did was give the associate an opportunity to correct any problems the customer may have had with the service. If, for example, the customer said at that time he did not feel he had received outstanding service, the associate could pursue the issue, find out why, and take corrective action.

It worked like a charm. So well, in fact, that the team got all sorts of recognition. And what do you think management's response to all this was? Well, their conclusion was that the reason the team's customer satisfaction rating had skyrocketed was because—in the main—of this new closing they had developed. So management immediately mandated that every associate on every team in every call center build the word "outstanding" into their closing.

And how did those other associates—the ones not on the "team"—react? They were livid. It was a stupid idea. Embarrassing. Just another "thing" management was ordering them to do—as if they didn't have enough to do already. If it had any effect at all, it was negative. Malicious compliance was the order of the day.

The most famous example was an associate who had been with the company for more than three years; incredible longevity in an industry that typically experienced turnover rates between fifty and one hundred percent. And he was highly rated, typically receiving top evaluations.

During a random monitoring session this employee was heard to tell a customer, "I understand we're supposed to have some bad weather today. I hope you don't get caught *out standing* in the rain."

Called to the carpet, the employee was admonished and a letter of rebuke was put in his file. But his disingenuous defense was that he had complied with management's instructions—he had built "outstanding" into his close.

Call Center Implementation Case Study: Analysis

Of course, management had unfortunately missed the point. It wasn't the "close" that the team had developed that had catapulted them into first place. It was the fact that they had been given the right to determine their own close. Self-determination was the catalyst, not the word "outstanding." Forcing others to use the same close had the exact opposite effect—it reduced self-determination, which, in turn, decreased employee engagement and led to disenchantment and, in some cases, dis-enfranchisement.

For the pilot team it was a direct application of the Golden Rule. They were treated the way management itself would like to be—no, would expect, maybe even demand to be—treated. And it worked wonders.

For the rest of the associates—those not on the pilot team who were "ordered" to use that same close—it was "same old, same old." Just another management directive to add to the pile.

This example is instructive from several points of view. First, all management asked of the team was that they be informed of what the team was doing. They didn't set up any sort of formal approval process. That automatically eliminated one of the main problems with typical employee empowerment programs—the flood of ideas that had to be evaluated. In this case, in essence, employees were evaluating their own suggestions, and eliminating many of them, so a formal, management-led approval process was not necessary.

Hence, the team members really felt as though they were "empowered," and, in fact, they were. This, of course, meant that the system they built intrinsically included a predisposition to say "yes," since the employees would obviously approve the suggestions that survived the filter of their own "approval" process.

It was successful also, I believe, because one of the "going-in" principles the team was asked to follow was that they focus on their own jobs, and not make suggestions as to what anyone else in the center or in the company ought to do. (In the past, most of the suggestions—that ultimately ended up in the "black hole"—had to do with recommended changes to the information systems. These typically would have required enormous amounts of time just to evaluate, let alone implement. And then there would be follow-on costs associated with possible linkages to other systems, retraining, and so on.) Following that principle was what enabled management to step aside and allow employees to essentially approve and implement their own suggestions.

But the effort ultimately didn't succeed as well as the isolated experience of this team might have suggested. Why? Primarily, I believe, because the company missed the third principle. They imposed an unnecessary standard. They made everyone essentially use the same close that this team had developed. It cost them time, money, and, ultimately, had the opposite of the intended effect.

It's the Process, not the Product

What propelled this team from fortieth to first place was not a new close; it was the fact they were "empowered" to develop their own new close—or whatever else they happened to focus on. It was management employing the GRL—

treating people the way they would like to be treated. It was the "process" of empowerment, not the "product" of those empowered ideas that was important. It was the newfound "control" they had over their lives that made the difference.

Implementation Case Study: Toyota

It's one thing to follow these principles when you're talking about a team of twenty associates, but what about a company with tens of thousands—or even hundreds of thousands—of employees? A company like Toyota. At forty-plus suggestions a year for more than two hundred thousand employees, Toyota fields more than eight million suggestions every year. How in the world do they do that, and how many people do they have in place to manage the process?

Let's address the second question first. They have no formal approval process, so there are essentially no people in place to manage a process that doesn't exist. So, then, how do they do it?

The managers of the process are the managers themselves—or team leaders, as Toyota calls them. Toyota is organized in a step-work of teams. Assembly workers on the line are formed into teams. (In fact, Toyota's employees are not called employees at all—they're called team members.) Each of those teams has a team leader. The team leaders, in turn, are formed into teams, and each of those teams of team leaders has a group leader. And so on up the line. Everyone is a member of a team.

The Toyota Production System

This organization is the historical evolution of the highly praised Toyota Production System,[19] which was developed by Taichi Ohno shortly after World War II. In 1949, Toyota was among the least productive of all the world's automakers—by Toyota's own admission the American automobile industry was eight to nine times more productive than they were.[20] The then head of Toyota, Kiichiro Toyoda (Toyoda in Japanese means "abundant rice field." The Toyoda family didn't feel that was a proper name for an automobile company, so they changed the "d" to a "t," and came up with Toyota, which has no meaning in Japanese)[21] issued a mandate that within three years Toyota would be the most productive automobile company in the world. And he assigned responsibility for accomplishing that to Ohno, his head of production.

Talk about a challenging vision! Just imagine the almost mind-boggling diffi-culty of that; increase productivity by a factor of almost ten in three years. How would you like to be given that responsibility? First order of the day, update your resume and get out—fast.

Making matters worse was the fact Toyota had a "no lay-off" policy. They had settled a bitter labor dispute in 1946 (workers had literally taken over several plants by force) by agreeing to worker demands for lifetime employment.[22] In return, Toyota received a pledge that workers would continually try to improve the company.

So Ohno had to accomplish this daunting feat without laying off a single employee. He began with a premise that Japanese workers in general, and Toyota workers in particular, were just as intelligent, just as talented, just as hard working as their European and American counterparts. Therefore, since the productivity "problem" was not the worker, it must be the work itself. Ohno reasoned that Toyota's work processes must be rife with waste and inefficiencies.

During the course of his efforts, to validate his premise and enhance his understanding, Ohno made a number of trips to the United States to study and learn from the American auto industry. The end product of his investigation and analysis was a three-pronged strategy focused on achieving one overarching objective: totally eliminate all waste and inefficiency. The objective and strategies are captured in the following illustration—the house that Ohno built.[23]

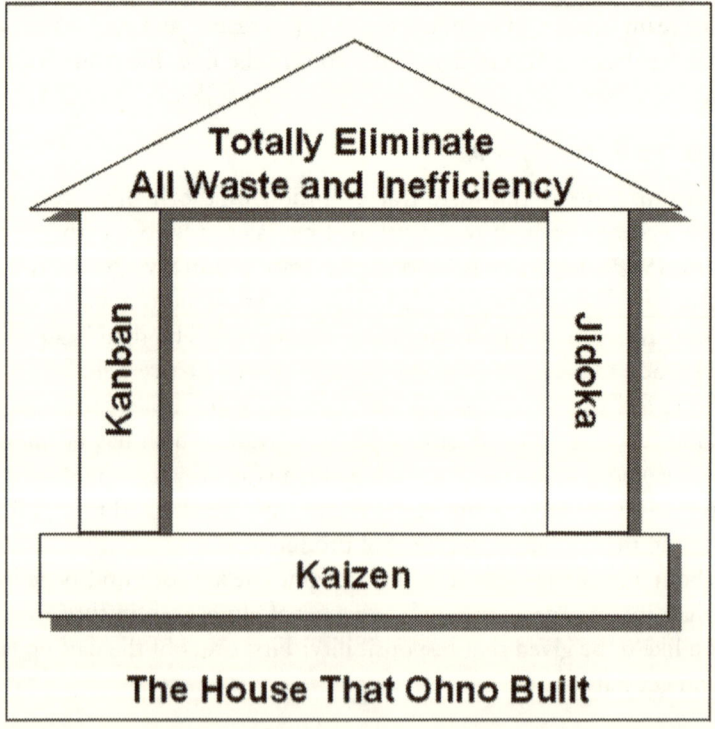

The House That Ohno Built

The overall objective, as illustrated above, was to totally eliminate all waste and inefficiency. Ohno reasoned that the primary cause of waste in a production process was excess inventory. Not inventory in and of itself, but *excess* inventory. A number of people have mistakenly referred to Toyota's production process as a "zero-inventory" process. Not so. Toyota has inventory at every step in the process; it just doesn't have excess inventory.

Kanban

Ohno's thought process was that excess inventory tended to hide the other problems in the plant. If, for example, a particular step in the process was producing defective parts, excess inventory could make up for it. If a particular step was lagging behind, the shortfall could be made up from excess inventory. And so on.

Ohno figured if you eliminated excess inventory, it would be like lowering the water level in a flooded room,—all the other problems would rise to the surface where they could be attacked and solved.

So he needed to develop a production process that would allow him to eliminate excess inventory. For his model he used what he called the "supermarket system," which he happened across when he stopped into a supermarket on his visit to the United States. After a customer took a product off the shelf in the store, an employee would replace it "just in time" for the next customer. Not literally in every case, of course. But that was the concept.

For some products—those on peg hooks, for example—there were actually reorder cards hanging at the back of the products on the same pegs. When the last product was picked by a customer, all the store had to do was send in the reorder card. In Ohno's view it was a simple, yet elegant communication system.

So the Kanban system was his manufacturing interpretation of the supermarket system. Unlike traditional production processes where every step on the line has a daily production quota, in Kanban only the last step—final assembly—has a quota. That quota then dictates production throughout the rest of the plant. Requirements wash backward like a wave through the plant. Essentially the way it works (simplified for illustration purposes) is that workers in final assembly walk back to the previous step and pick the parts, components and sub-assemblies they need to complete the production of the automobile they're working on. They leave behind a kanban, a sign card—the equivalent of that reorder card on the peg hook in the supermarket—that tells workers on that previous step what they took.

Those workers then use that kanban as their production quota. They, in turn, go to the previous step in the process and pick the parts, components and sub-assemblies they need to replace the items that were taken from them to be used by final assembly, and they, too, leave behind a kanban. And so on. This process continues to cascade backward through the plant with each step receiving its production instructions from the following step.

That's at dramatic odds with traditional manufacturing processes where every step on the line has a production quota. That's where the excess inventory comes from. Every step is producing, not to meet customer demand, but to meet an artificial quota, established more to ensure worker productivity than plant productivity. A classic example of sub-optimization.

Jidoka

Jidoka is Toyota's technology strategy. Many people mistakenly credit Toyota's mind-boggling productivity figures to an assumed pervasive use of technology. In fact, Toyota is probably among the least automated of any automobile company. Their basic philosophy is that technology limits flexibility and innovation and, therefore, should be used only when there are clear advantages.

Contrast Toyota's situation with General Motors'. At the beginning of the 1980s, GM had a breathtaking forty-six percent share of the automotive market in this country. But they had begun to feel the early effects of the Japanese juggernaut. Toyota, and other Japanese car companies, were producing higher quality cars for less money and selling them at lower prices.

In an attempt to catapult GM into the forefront of automobile companies when it came to productivity and quality, General Motors launched *GM10,* a technology-intensive strategy. Over the next decade, GM invested billions[24] to automate their plants and achieve their vision of productivity and quality leadership. But by the end of the decade, GM's domestic market share had dropped dramatically,[25] and it still had not realized its vision.

The interesting thing is GM's strategy was successfully implemented. By the end of the decade, GM's plants were probably the most automated in the world. The problem wasn't implementation; it was that the strategy was fundamentally flawed from the start.

When the market shifted from large gas-guzzling luxury cars to small, fuel-efficient vehicles and back again, GM was unable to easily make the transitions. It would have required additional massive investments to apply still more automation and/or reconfigure existing systems. In the end, GM was not fully ready to respond to shifts in consumer preferences, and its market share suffered.

Toyota, on the other hand, never went the automation route. Their strategy all along was to rely on process innovations driven by frontline employees to improve quality and productivity. When changes in consumer preferences came along, it was much easier to retrain people than it would have been to replace or update technology.

Principles of *Jidoka*

That, of course, does not mean Toyota does not have a technology strategy; it does. At its most fundamental level, *Jidoka* says two things. First, design all machines so they stop automatically if they encounter any sort of abnormality. That means Toyota does not have to have a team member "tending" every machine all the time (as is the case in many manufacturers). Rather, a worker only has to intervene if the machine stops, a clear and unambiguous signal that the machine needs attention for some reason. The productivity advantages in Toyota's approach are obvious.

The second principle underlying *Jidoka* is that good technology should never be applied to bad process. Fix the process first, then apply technology, if necessary, to affect further improvements. Basically that says that at Toyota, technology is a solution of last-resort, not first-resort—a dramatic departure from traditional thinking.

And it works. Consistently. Toyota clearly leads the pack in profit per employee, a key productivity measure. And, in spite of the recession in the early 2000s, its sales during the past five years have increased by more than $42 billion—more than twice the increase of any other automobile company. Its profits have been rock-steady too; during that same period they totaled more than $33 billion, over fifty percent more than any other automobile company.

The key, of course, to all this, is the third prong of Ohno's strategy, and the foundation for Toyota's success: Kaizen.

Kaizen[26]

Kaizen, or continuous improvement, is Toyota's "people" strategy—the third prong and foundation of Ohno's vaunted Toyota Production System. The roots of kaizen go back to the deal Toyota made with its employees to end the labor dispute shortly after World War II. Remember, the employees had agreed to work to continuously improve Toyota.

The heart of kaizen's implementation is in the very definition of a job at Toyota. At most companies, an employee's job is to execute the functions of their job. It's a circular definition. Your job is to do your job. At Toyota that's also partially true. But there's more. Employees are not only expected to do their jobs, they are also expected to find ways to do them better, faster, easier, cheaper, etc. In effect, they are expected to innovate improvements in their jobs.

Toyota's entire business is built around this seemingly simple concept. When, for example, a potential employee applies to Toyota, the first step in the hiring process is not an interview. Rather, applicants are brought into a simulated plant environment and taught how to perform a typical job—installing the spare tire, for example. After they've learned the basics of the job, they actually go ahead and perform it for a period of time. Toyota is looking for two things. First, do they have the coordination and strength to perform the job? After all, many jobs at an automobile plant are physically demanding.

And second, do they have the capacity to innovate improvements? So, after they've performed the job for a while, they are then interviewed and asked a series of questions, including things like, "Did they enjoy the work?" and so on. But the key question is, "Can you think of ways to improve the job to make it easier, or faster, or simpler, or less time-consuming?" If the interviewee cannot think of any possible improvements, they are removed from the potential applicant pool.

Once they're on the job, employees are asked to constantly focus on three things: simplify, combine or eliminate. That is, can you think of any way to simplify what you're doing, or perhaps combine it with an upstream or downstream function? Or maybe even eliminate it entirely? That's the essence of Toyota's focus on improvements. Easy to understand. Easy to carry out. Easy to implement.

The results, as we stated earlier, speak for themselves. Roughly forty suggestions per employee per year. Mostly small, since the suggestions are focused on the employees' own jobs. But the aggregate effect is huge. It's the GRL applied with a clear win-win effect: (1) Management treats team members as they themselves (i.e., management) would like to be treated. Hence, team members feel valued and they, in turn, make suggestions that are subsequently implemented. And (2) Toyota experiences a significant increase in efficiency and productivity, and a concomitant decrease in cost. That, in turn, allows them to hold the line on—or even reduce—prices, which, in turn, allows them to be more competitive in the marketplace.

Kaizen: A Competitive Force

The question a lot of people have is, despite the clear advantages to the company, why would people work to improve their jobs, given those guidelines? If an employee, for example, were to "eliminate" what they do, wouldn't they also, by definition, eliminate their own job?

In theory, I suppose that could be true. But remember the other half of the 1946 agreement with the workers? Lifetime employment. That's the "safety net" that allows employees to feel comfortable making suggestions to simplify, combine or eliminate their job functions.

Toyota's theory has always been that the purpose of the improvements is not to "downsize," but rather to make Toyota a leaner, meaner competitor. So Toyota doesn't use these improvements as an opportunity to get rid of people. After all, why would you want to get rid of someone who is clever enough and innovative enough to figure out ways to improve his or her job, and, by extension, the company? That's exactly the type of person you want working for you.

No, Toyota uses these improvements to improve quality, cut costs (for example, by reducing the need to hire additional employees, rather than by cutting existing headcount), and make Toyota vehicles even more competitive so they can increase revenues and profits. Ultimately, the net effect of that, of course, is probably a need to add employees as demand increases.

Here is just one example of the dramatic operational differences this philosophy makes. The mantra in automobile plants since the industry began has been, "Don't stop the line!" The theory, of course, is if you stop the line you reduce yield (the number of cars actually produced divided by the number scheduled to be produced), which reduces productivity, which increases costs, which means you have to charge a higher price, which means the vehicles could potentially be less attractive on the market. If there is a defect or a quality problem in any step on the line, the theory is that it can be corrected in rework (which is where all the problems that have been built into the cars during the normal production process are corrected). The theoretical target is a one hundred percent yield. That is, most plants hope to actually produce what the production plan has called for.

In reality, ninety percent is "…often considered a sign of good management."[27] Why? All sorts of reasons. Production glitches. Inventory shortages. Equipment breakdowns. All kinds of normal problems most plants experience.

Toyota's Approach

At Toyota they have a different mantra: "Don't pass a problem on to the next step in the line!" That means if the line has to stop to avoid passing a problem on, so be it. Better to correct the problem once and avoid building it into every succeeding vehicle, than to just pass it on and have to correct all the vehicles in rework.

The net result: Toyota, with its "stop the line whenever you have to" philosophy, regularly hits a ninety-five percent yield. In fact, if that number starts to trend higher, team leaders begin to get nervous. They're concerned that some problems may be being passed on, which will create rework issues and potential quality problems.

An interesting, albeit unfortunate, sidelight to this is when a group of employees from another automobile company toured a Toyota-run plant and were later asked what they thought of it, their response was, at best, unenthusiastic. When pressed for explanations about their reaction, the general answer was, in effect, that it was not a "real" plant.[28]

Of course, the interviewer probed deeper, trying to understand what was behind this incongruous statement—after all, the plant did, in fact, produce automobiles. And the automobiles were of the highest quality! Essentially the thing that so confounded the touring visitors was Toyota's rework area, or, more precisely, the lack thereof.

The concept of rework is so deeply ingrained in the culture and history of most automobile companies that the mere thought of doing without one almost goes against nature. Upwards of 20% of the floor space in a typical "Western" automobile factory is dedicated to rework.[29] At Toyota, it's a mere fraction of that.

Eliminate Unnecessary Standards

The other paradigm shift that confounds observers of Toyota's remarkable success is the issue of standards. Automobile plants are among the most structured operations in the world. If an employee on the line figures out a way to simplify, combine or eliminate his or her job function, then doesn't everyone who does that job have to implement that same improvement? And, if so, since most improvements are small, wouldn't the cost of updating all the operations manuals, retraining the workers, and implementing the change across the company far exceed the benefit of that change?

Not surprisingly, Toyota's philosophy regarding standards is different from most. Standards are mandated only if absolutely necessary. So, for example, technology systems are standardized across the company. (Which is one of the reasons Toyota eschews the use of technology unless it's shown to be of dramatic benefit. It tends to build inflexibility into the system, which, in turn, stifles innovation—the key to Toyota's success.)

So different Toyota plants evolve differently, based on employee suggestions and innovations. For example, the Toyota plant in Georgetown, Kentucky, when it was first built, was an exact replica of Toyota's plant in Toyota City in Japan. The square footage, the floor layout, even the equipment. Toyota actually had to go back to manufacturers and have them build out-of-date models of equipment so it would match what they had in Toyota City.

The assembly line procedures and processes were identical. When the doors were opened in Georgetown, you couldn't see the difference between there and the Toyota City plant, except that the workers spoke English rather than Japanese.

After only a few years, however, the plants were dramatically different, and, if you looked at the details of each operation, you would have been hard pressed to find similarities. Why? Because the suggestions that were made—and implemented—in the two plants were different.

But how about within the same plant? Surely assembly line workers performing the same task in the same plant should do it the same way. Doesn't that create essentially the same problem, just on a smaller scale? That is, even the cost of changing standards in the same plant, redoing operations manuals, retraining employees, and so on, would far exceed the small benefit of most suggestions.

That's probably true. But, again, Toyota has a different philosophy from most companies. The culture is built around suggestions and recognition for those suggestions. The dollar rewards are not great—a few dollars is typical. The recognition really valued by the employees is a simple certificate that the team member can post in his or her work area. The more certificates, the greater the prestige and peer recognition. So everyone wants to earn more certificates.

Here's how it works. At Toyota, the philosophy is that a copied suggestion is of equal value to an original suggestion. That runs counter to what most of us have been brought up to believe. In school, for example, copying was a "no-no." Detention, or worse, was the most likely outcome if copying were discovered. At Toyota, it's just the opposite. Copying is encouraged and rewarded.

So let's say Sally, a fictitious employee, comes up with an idea for a small improvement in her job, and she makes a suggestion. Now we are faced with the problem. Investing the time and person-hours to analyze the idea will, in and of itself, probably cost more than the benefit of the suggestion. But then we also have the cost of introducing the change to the rest of the organization, retraining the employees who do the same job Sally does, dealing with resistance and potential malicious compliance, and so on. Hardly worth the effort. In fact, not worth the effort.

Perhaps, but that's not the way it works at Toyota. To continue our little hypothetical example, let's say Sally is having lunch with Charlie, a co-worker who performs the same function she does. Sally is excited about her idea and tells Charlie about it. He runs back to his work area after lunch, writes up exactly the same suggestion, submits it, and gets a certificate.

"Foul!" you might cry. "That's stealing. Charlie doesn't deserve the certificate! He stole the idea from Sally!" That's exactly right. And Charlie knows it. And so does Sally. And so do Sally's and Charlie's team leaders. And that's exactly what they want. Because that's how "standards" get updated. Not by mandate, but by a cultural imperative to make, implement and share suggestions for improvement. The idea, of course, as Sally, Charlie, and all their fellow team members and team leaders know, is that tomorrow, or the next day, or next week, Charlie will have an idea that he will share with Sally, and she will copy it and get her certificate. And so on.

The cost to Toyota: basically zero. The employees take care of it themselves. Many, if not most, ideas are actually implemented before the suggestion sheet is submitted. Team leaders are there more as sounding boards than anything else, to help team members think through their ideas, to help by asking questions, and occasionally—but rarely—to challenge an idea based on cost.

So that's Toyota, with perhaps the best and most comprehensive employee engagement process in the world. But what about the rest of us? After all, Toyota's been at it for more than fifty years; it's not surprising they have the process pretty well mastered. How do we get started?

Toyota and the GRL

Before addressing that question, let's return to the GRL. If you "peel back the onion" on the Toyota Production System (TPS) what you find is that it's nothing more than a comprehensive, all-encompassing application of the Golden Rule of Leadership. Fundamental to Toyota's success is a basic belief in the value of employees. They, not systems, not organization structures, not technology, not management, not anything else, are what drive Toyota's quality and productivity. And the manifestation of that belief in the value of employees is the fact that they are treated, quite simply, as human beings. As you or I might like to be treated in similar circumstances.

With that overarching thought in mind, there are two basic approaches to employee engagement systems: principles-based and process-based. Both can work, and both carry their own benefits and challenges.

Principles-Based Employee Engagement

Basically this is the Toyota approach. It's an approach that relies not only on the support of senior management, but their active involvement as well. It's pervasive, involving everyone in the organization.

The idea is to develop a set of principles (hopefully just a few) on which to base employee engagement. And then to use those principles to guide the efforts throughout the organization.

We mentioned Toyota's. A predisposition to say "yes," focus on your own job, and don't mandate unnecessary standards. It seems to me those are as good a place as any to start, but there may be others, or different ones, you wish to use in your own organization.

A Key "Watch-Out"

One "watch-out" is how you deal with ideas that eliminate jobs. Toyota's philosophy has always been that the ultimate goal is to increase business, not reduce the number of jobs, so employees are confident that their efforts will not result in their being laid off.

But they have a fifty-plus year history to rely on. If you're just getting started, employees may not be as confident their jobs will be protected. So you may have to incorporate a principle that explicitly protects their jobs. "No one will improve him or herself out of a job," for example. That allows the business to make head-count adjustments while at the same time protect those employees who are actively attempting to improve the business.

This "principles-based" approach also implies some potentially massive changes throughout the organization. For example, like Toyota, you may want to build the idea of capacity for continuous improvement into your recruitment and selection processes. Training may be required to help existing employees make the transition to the "new way of doing business." And the sad reality is that some people—potentially including members of management—may need to be replaced if they can't adjust to the new environment.

Process-based Employee Engagement

This is a fundamentally different approach. Unlike principles-based, which is, in effect, woven into the very fabric of the organization, process-based engagement can be implemented on a much more limited basis. In that sense, its potential is somewhat more limited as well. But it does have some advantages. For example, it doesn't rely on the active support and involvement of senior management, so it can be done at any level in the organization, including the first line.

Basically it's a variation on the old "quality circle" theme, where improvement teams are set up to deal with a specific issue. Typically their "empowerment" is more limited. They usually have to make suggestions to management, who will then, in turn, approve or disapprove them. But they can make some dramatic improvements, and the employees who participate on them tend to really "get into it."

A Case Example

Important improvements can come out of a process-based employee engagement system. I worked with a client on just such an initiative. It was a pilot project involving a frontline group of installation, maintenance and repair (IMR) "techs." The manager who had been picked to lead the effort was a crusty thirty-plus year veteran, and people actually warned me that he would be more of an impediment than a help, and that he may actually "get in the way" of success. Not exactly ideal conditions to begin such a project.

But it turned out that "people" were wrong. The manager was wonderful. He selected a team composed of five or six techs and one supervisor, and we held a "kick-off" meeting. After I spent some time explaining what we were trying to do, how it would work, and so on—and after the employees had a chance to ask questions—the manager stood up and "took the floor."

<u>The Challenge</u>

He told the group they could come up with any suggestions they wanted to, and talk about any area they wanted to focus on. All he asked was that they give him some ideas about what to do about the "missed commitment" problem, an issue everyone was well aware of.

Missed commitments were a key measure both operationally and in terms of customer satisfaction. The way it worked was that when a customer called in—whether it was for a new order, or maintenance or repairs on existing equipment—the company would commit to a specific time that that customer's request would be satisfied.

Let's say, for example, that a customer calls in with an "out-of-service" problem, and the company commits they will have the customer back in service by 7:00 p.m., that same day. If, in fact, the customer is back in service at 7:02 p.m., the company has missed the commitment.

There were broad implications to these missed commitments, both internally and externally. Clearly there were customer satisfaction issues that concerned the company—poor customer satisfaction could become a public relations issue and potentially open the door to competition. And since this company was in a regulated industry, customer satisfaction was not just a competitive issue. They were under the watchful eye of a public utility commission (PUC) that looked askance at things like missed commitments. Problems in this area could create issues for the company when they applied for rate increases and so on.

Well, back to our intrepid team and our kick-off meeting. The group accepted the challenge. Their final question was when they would be allowed to meet, and for how long. The manager's response, "You tell me. This is your project. Run it any way you want."

They were literally blown away. Speechless. This was a union shop. They were accustomed to operating under strict guidelines. It was unheard of for them to have the authority to do something like this. In my opinion, it was those three little words—you tell me—that set the stage for the success of this team and for the pilot project.

The team responded to the challenge and within two weeks, missed commitments had been literally cut in half. A fifty percent improvement in two weeks on a metric that they had been wrestling with—with very little to show for their efforts—literally for years, even decades. How in the world did they accomplish that?

The Solution

Here's what they did. They tried to figure out why there was a problem, and they came up with two fundamental and interrelated reasons. The first was that techs were either not aware of the commitment time, or were so busy they simply did not pay attention to it. They worked a job as fast as they could, and then moved on to the next.

So, for example, they might complete the job (i.e., have the customer back in service) in the above example by 6:55 p.m., and then proceed to pack up their equipment and load their truck. All this could easily take five or ten minutes, or even longer. Then they would call in the job completion—in our example, at 7:02 p.m. A job completed on time that went into the books as a missed commitment. So, they reasoned, their first challenge was simply getting people to focus on the commitment time.

But the second related issue was what happened when the commitment was missed. From the techs' perspective—nothing. The supervisor had to write up the "missed commitment" report, and those reports were filed away. Unless there was an egregious problem, or if a tech had a particularly bad "missed commitment" record (which was rare—it was really a pervasive, company-wide issue), nothing more came of it—at least from the techs' perspective. The company, of course, still had all the customer, public relations and PUC issues to deal with.

So what did the team do? They surmised the primary reason techs were not "tuned in" to the commitment time was precisely because there were no negative after-effects. Missed commitments were simply "something that went with the territory." Everybody—including management—was too busy to get too worked up about missing commitments when they had huge backlogs and scarce resources.

So the team recommended a very simple solution. They suggested the techs be required to write up the missed commitment reports themselves. That way, if they missed a commitment, there was an after-effect. They'd have to write up one of those "stupid" reports, something they had no desire to do. Avoiding that became a priority for the techs, so they began to focus on commitment times. All of a sudden, missed commitments for silly reasons—like packing up equipment and loading the truck before calling in the job completion—went away. Those silly reasons, as it turned out, were a primary cause of missed commitments.

Think about how amazing this recommended solution was. These were union employees recommending they be given more work to do—that is, writing up a report. Have you ever run across anything like that before?

And think about how simple, yet elegant the solution was. No elaborate systems or processes had to be developed and implemented. No broad-based monitoring and control system had to be put in place. No system of rewards and punishments. Just a simple and relatively minor shift of responsibility.

The Lesson

And why did it work so well? Because it was the employees themselves who suggested it. First of all, it probably would never have occurred to management to suggest this type of solution. (In fact, it almost certainly had never occurred to management—after all, they'd been dealing with this issue for decades, and never come up with this solution.) But just imagine what would have happened had management come along and told the union that they now had to write-up the missed commitment reports. It's not too difficult to envision a scenario that includes grievances and possible work stoppages.

The bottom line is that if you give employees an opportunity to use their brains as well as their arms and legs, they will amaze you with their inventiveness and creativity. If you give them an opportunity to have some control over what they do and how they do it, they will astound you with their commitment, dedication and hard work. If you treat people the way you would like to be treated, they will respond the way you would respond.

Control and self-determination—that's what it's all about.

Getting Started—Think GRL

So how do you go about getting started? There are some similarities in the approach, whether you choose principles-based or process-based, but there are some differences as well. In either case, it's essential the employees be involved in the design and development of the system, and not just its implementation. After all, they are the ones who will be most impacted by what happens, and they are the ones who are closest to the situation—it only makes sense to give them a voice in the process. Again, think GRL.

Before embarking on a principles-based approach, it's essential to checkpoint senior management's commitment to the effort. And here's the "rub." Just about every senior manager today knows exactly what to say, knows the "right words" when it comes to employee involvement (or empowerment, or engagement). So it's very difficult to know whether there is true commitment, or merely "lip service," no matter how well intentioned.

By the way, there is no intent in the above paragraph to denigrate senior management or to cast aspersions on their intentions. I worked with a company where senior management was the driving force behind a principles-based effort, and they backed up their commitment with time, people and money. But they didn't really know what they were in for. It wasn't long before the employees' thinking had eclipsed that of senior management, and those senior managers actually began to get in the way of progress.

Picture an oval track where senior management fires the starter's pistol and takes off, encouraging the employees to follow. At first, senior management takes the lead and is way ahead. But before long, when senior management figuratively looks over their left shoulder to see how the employees are doing, they zoom by on the right, lapping senior management. The next time senior management looks back, they see the employees and assume that they're still behind them when, in fact, they're about to "lap" senior management for a second time.

So senior management is busy trying to direct efforts when the employees have long since solved those problems and are working on more advanced issues. Senior management and the employees both assume that the other isn't listening, or, perhaps, isn't hearing. The result: a powerful disconnect. Senior management then decides to assert its authority, steps in and mandates that what they're saying be followed, and that can ultimately derail the initiative.

That's not a criticism of senior management, it's simply a recognition of reality. When it comes to a principles-based approach, nobody really knows what they're in for because there are far-reaching implications that touch virtually every part of the business, including the culture.

For that reason, I recommend that any employee engagement effort—whether principles-based or process-based—begin with a pilot, or, better yet, multiple pilots. Apply the GRL. Allow the employees to develop the different approaches that will be used in the various pilots. The multiple pilots and approaches will allow the organization to figure out what works and what doesn't work, to better understand the types of problems and obstacles they'll face, and to determine the best approach to overcome those impediments.

Most importantly, the total effort will have the backing of the employees because it will have been the employees who participated in the development and implementation of the pilots, and in the post-pilot debriefs and analysis. They will have a sense of ownership, of pride. They will have a commitment and dedication to make it work across the organization.

Here are a few ideas about "process-based" pilots you may want to think about.

After Action Review (AAR)

This is the approach the U.S. Army took when it was essentially—and successfully—trying to reinvent itself. Basically what they do, at the conclusion of any given undertaking, is conduct an AAR to capture the learnings. AARs are built around three simple questions: What did we set out to do? What did we actually do? And why was there a difference?

That third question actually breaks down into four sub-questions: What worked? What didn't work, or, in effect, what didn't turn out the way we had hoped or expected it to? What should we do differently next time? And what are our overarching learnings from this experience?

Who's involved in these AARs? Anyone who was involved in the effort under review. That means, in the case of the army, frontline soldiers as well as the commanding officers directly responsible for—and involved in—whatever the effort was. The key points are captured and passed on to others who may be involved in similar undertakings.

So what's the corporate equivalent of the army's AAR? I think it can be very similar. And I think it can be employed by intact work groups as well as project teams. The process can be virtually identical to what the army does. Simply pull the group together and, in a very structured fashion, walk through the following questions:

AAR Questions

1. What did we set out to do—what was our objective?

2. What did we actually do—did we accomplish what we had hoped to?

3. What worked—what did we do right?

4. What didn't work as well as we would have liked—what could be improved?

5. What should we do differently in the future?

6. Are there any other "lessons" that we need to capture from this experience and build into future undertakings?

The After Action Review

Depending upon the complexity of what the group is working on, this process can typically be done in one to two hours. The critical point, of course, is to ensure that the suggestions made actually get implemented. It's also important—for the integrity of the AAR process itself—that the review be nonjudgmental, especially when it comes to question number four. If people feel they are going to be disciplined—or even perhaps embarrassed—in any way, they will be very reluctant to admit to having done anything wrong, or to suggest anything needs to be improved.

Suggestions, too, need to be accepted without criticism. The quickest and easiest way to "kill" an AAR is by critiquing each suggestion that is made. For example, "Oh, we've tried that before, and it doesn't work." "That isn't the way we do things around here." Or, even more directly, "Come on, get with it, that's a stupid idea." These comments, and comments like them, will quickly put an end to the AAR and people will simply stop talking.

Once all the suggestions are made, the group can go back and evaluate them to determine which they want to implement. But even here the focus should be on the positive, not the negative. Select the ideas you want to pursue. There's no need to disparage those that were not selected.

Functional Improvement Team (FIT)

A second possible pilot is to pull together a group of people who work in the same area (although they don't necessarily have to be part of the same intact work group), and ask them to help develop ways to improve a specific area. A good example is the installation, maintenance and repair (IMR) team I described earlier. Although they had a broader mandate, think about their efforts in regard to the missed commitments issue. That's the idea.

Narrow Scope

For best results, the focus of the group, I believe, should be relatively narrow—something within their area of responsibility. And, like the IMR group, it's best to give them a lot of latitude in the way they approach the issue.

Management Support

Management's role here is to be supportive of the group's efforts, to give them the time they need to focus on the issue, and to have a "predisposition to say 'yes.'" That doesn't mean that management can't—or shouldn't—ask relevant questions and try to re-focus the group if the effort seems to be getting off track, or if the focus of a recommended solution involves the expenditure of lots of money. In those cases management clearly needs to step in, but gently. (And remember the racetrack metaphor—make sure you're not the one who's off-track before mandating changes.)

Budget Awareness—Upfront

In fact, if money is a big issue (which it is almost everywhere and in almost every case), management should set that as a guideline up front. You don't want people to feel as though they've been "tricked" in any way. Just tell them that budgets are limited and they need to look for solutions that can be implemented for very little, or no, money. They'll understand the money issue. More than likely they've been living with it for some time, just as you have. And I think you'll find they're likely to be even more creative and inventive in their solutions with the money guideline in place.

Don't "Steer" the Team

One watch-out is a common temptation of management to "steer" the team away from solutions which they—management—believes won't work. Even if something apparently identical to the group's recommendation has been tried before, it may not have been the product of a suggestion by an employee group, and, therefore, may not have had the same degree of buy-in and ownership by the employees that the current suggestion may have. Plus, if you "kill it," no matter how gently, the group will feel as though they've only been put together to keep guessing at solutions until they've hit the one you've already decided on—a classic "rock-fetching" exercise. (You know, "Is this the rock you wanted? No, then how about this one? This one? All right, come on, just tell us which one you want.")

Cross-functional Improvement Team (CFIT)

A third alternative is to pull together a group of people from different functional areas who work on different steps in the same process. Of course this requires the cooperation of different managers, and that makes it a little more difficult to do. But it can, potentially, yield the most valuable results.

Case Example: The Situation

I worked with a utility company that had major disconnects all along the way in their customer order fulfillment process. The way it worked (in somewhat simplified fashion) was that the customer would call in an order to Customer Service, who would then commit to a completion date based on company standards. The order was then sent to Analysis to determine if the necessary facilities and equipment were in place to provide the service. Assuming that some work had to be done, the order would then be sent to Systems for whatever engineering was required, and then to Plant for construction or upgrading of facilities and equipment. Finally, the order would be sent to Dispatch, who would then contact Operations for installation.

Often the completion date committed to the customer was missed. This, of course, set off all sorts of red flags and alarms. Customer satisfaction was at risk. The PUC could get involved. Negative PR was a possibility. And so on.

And the natural—almost inevitable—outgrowth of all that was a classic finger-pointing exercise. Customer service made a bad commitment. The order didn't get sent to Analysis in a timely fashion. Analysis took too long. Engineering took too long. Plant took too long. And on and on and on.

Trying to fix the "blame" in any one given situation was a fruitless exercise. All the groups had become pretty expert at covering themselves. The company realized, however, that "fixing the blame" was the wrong approach; they wanted to "fix the problem." And, in the aggregate, it was clear that there was a systemic breakdown somewhere.

The Solution Process

We were brought in to do two things. First, try to identify shortcomings in the process and put a plan in place to fix them. And second, get the employees more engaged, more focused on serving the customer than on pointing the finger.

To do that we brought together a group of associates—frontline employees—from four of the key functions in the process. Each function was represented by four associates and, even though they had regular contact with each other by phone during the normal course of business, they had never met each other. It was clear from the outset that, while everyone was civil and polite, there was an undercurrent of personal animus that ran through the group—probably a result of the all-too-frequent "blame game" played by the participants.

We spent a couple of hours teaching the group how to map and analyze a process, and gave them some practice. Then we divided them into three subgroups, each of which included at least one person from each of the four functions. We asked them to (a) map three different versions of the customer fulfillment process, (b) identify opportunities for improvement, and (c) develop an action plan to take advantage of those opportunities.

All the groups performed in a stellar fashion. They did exactly as instructed and came up with some amazingly innovative ideas that would not only improve the process, but that would go a long way toward solving the "finger-pointing" problem.

Interestingly, though, those outstanding results were not the main benefit of the session. Almost to a person as they left the session, the associates said virtually the same thing to me. It went something like, "You know, I've worked with Charlie (or Sally, or whomever) for years, but I'd never actually met him before. He's a pretty good egg."

It's a lot easier to dislike—and point fingers at—a faceless voice on the phone than a real living breathing person that you have personal contact with.

I stayed in contact with the group for some time after the session, and they did implement many of the suggestions that they had come up with. But, not surprisingly given the reaction of the participants at the end of the session, the real value was in the improved interpersonal relationships that facilitated the entire business process.

Each of these suggested pilots would fall under the category of a "process-based" employee engagement program. I believe that's the best place for virtually any organization to begin. Like anything else, there's a learning curve associated with employee engagement, and you have to go through all the steps. Pilots like these give you, I believe, the best opportunity to advance up that curve in an orderly fashion with the added bonus of actually generating benefits along the way. Once the concept has been proven to senior management's satisfaction, and once they have bought into the idea of—and pledged their support for—a "principles-based" approach, you can more confidently move forward in that direction.

The Golden Rule

And let's not forget the GRL. How does that play into this whole process of employee engagement?

Well, the answer is probably pretty obvious from the above narrative, but let's make the implicit explicit. If you were an employee, how would you like to be treated? What would engage you?

More than likely you would want to be respected. To be valued for your contribution to the company. And to be recognized for your achievements. And you'd like to be treated for who you are—a person with brains, with intelligence, with knowledge, with experience. The question is, how does the company (i.e., your manager, since he or she is, in effect, the "company" to you) manifest that respect, that value, that recognition? How does he or she take advantage of your brains, knowledge, etc.?

I think it's probably fair to say that you'd want more than mere lip service—one of the most prevalent, even if inadvertent, manifestations of employee engagement. You wouldn't want to be merely asked for your "input," only to watch management go off and make all the decisions in your absence, not provide you with any information or explanation about what they thought of your suggestion or how they arrived at their decision, and then come back the next day and ask for more input.

Employees have figured that one out. That's not engagement, it's a mere pretense of engagement—perhaps a well-intentioned pretense, but a pretense nonetheless. Engagement isn't about input, it's about involvement. It's about control. It's about self-determination. It's about having a say in what you do and how you do it.

That's what you'd want, isn't it. Some control. Some say in how you discharge your responsibilities. So treat people the way you would like to be treated. Give employees more than input, give them some control. It is certainly management's prerogative to set objectives. But giving people a say in how they go about accomplishing those objectives yields enormous benefits, not only in the enhanced self-image and self-respect of the employees—which goes a long way toward employee satisfaction—but what they think of the company. Employees who know their own jobs better than anyone will more than likely come up with better ways to do it than you could. So there are potentially all sorts of productivity, effectiveness and efficiency benefits to be had as well.

Step 6: Energize the People—Key Points Summary

A. Business performance is a function of having satisfied customers. Satisfied customers are a function of operational excellence and engaged employees. And those, in turn, are a function of high-quality leadership.

B. To be truly engaged, employees must have an opportunity to be "involved," and not just to provide "input."

C. There are three primary reasons why companies have failed in their efforts to truly engage employees:

1. Companies often don't have the time, people or money to handle the volume of suggestions they get.

2. Employees typically don't have a broad enough perspective to make useful and meaningful suggestions.

3. Even when employee suggestions have been realistic, they haven't been "implementable" because the time and cost of creating a new "standard" that incorporates the suggestion far exceeds the benefit they get from that suggestion.

D. Toyota has overcome these challenges by implementing an employee engagement system based on three key principles:

1. Team leaders must have a predisposition to say "yes."

2. Employees must focus on their own jobs when they make suggestions.

3. Unnecessary standards should not be imposed.

E. The other basic approach to employee engagement systems is "process-based." There are a wide variety of possible implementation strategies, including the After Action Review, the Functional Improvement Team, and the Cross-Functional Improvement Team.

F. Remember, it is the "process" of empowerment, not the "product" of those empowered ideas that is important.

A Call to Action

Knowing is not enough; we must apply. Willing is not enough; we must do.

Johann von Goethe

So we've now come full circle. The question is no longer, "What's the secret of leadership?" The simple reality is there is no secret. Everything we need to know about leadership has been known for at least three thousand years. It's captured in the GRL: Treat other people the way you would like to be treated.

The question now is, "So what do we do now?" A good question because absent a specific commitment on our part to take action—to apply the GRL—this has all been an academic exercise.

Just to do a quick reset, leadership is about people and change—about leading people through change. The "people" part is captured in the application of the Golden Rule of Leadership. The "change" part is captured in what we have previously called the Leadership Process, six "things" leaders must do to effect change:

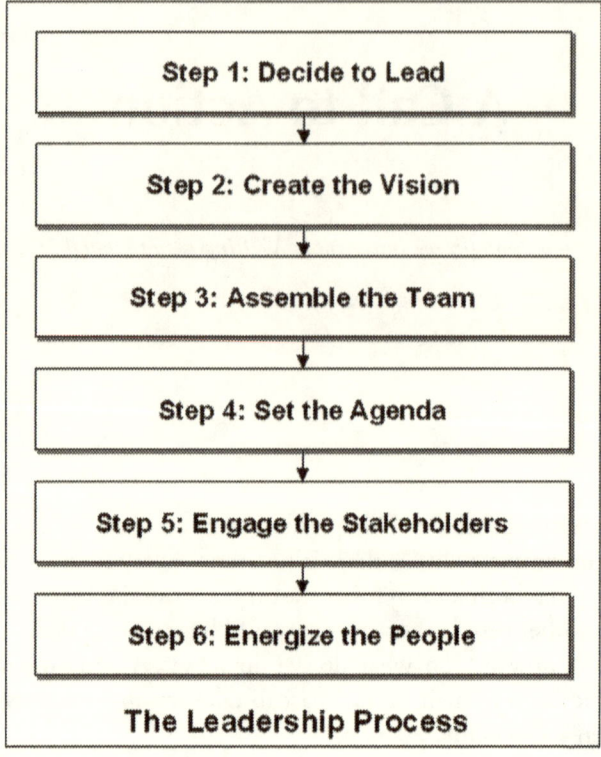

This process is not the only one. Remember the 9,000 books on leadership? There are lots of alternatives. But whatever process you choose, remember that that process—any process—is constantly evolving. And, regardless of what it is, remember that the "process," is, frankly, the easy part. It's relatively simple and straightforward—just another process we need to execute. And, if it were not for the "people" part of the challenge, anyone could do it.

That "people" part is the tough part. Conceptually, it's very straightforward—simply apply the GRL. But the application of the concept is far more difficult. It's not mysterious. It's not secret. But it is difficult.

But, like anything else, it can be successfully learned and applied by just about anyone. What it really takes is commitment. Commitment to become a more effective leader. Commitment to really care about people. Commitment to the Golden Rule—to treat others as you would like to be treated. Commitment to set aside our sometimes petty, but all too human feelings about—and disagreements with—others, and work hard to "keep our eyes on the prize."

With that, I'm suggesting a four-phase "call to action" for enhancing our own personal leadership.

A Call to Action

Phase I: Make the commitment

Without this, the rest is meaningless because it simply won't happen. Make the commitment to become a more effective leader. Make the commitment to truly care about people. Make the commitment to treat others the way you would like to be treated. That's the foundation for the rest of the plan.

Phase II: "Pilot" the GRL

Like anything else, there is a learning curve associated with the GRL. Wherever you happen to be—in some objective sense—on some overarching "average" GRL learning curve, assume you're at the bottom of your own personal learning curve. That's not intended to be a value judgment or a criticism. That's simply the way learning curves work. Any time you embark on a learning adventure, you start at the beginning, and the beginning is where you are now.

Remember, too, that the early phase of the learning curve is a slow one (see illustration).

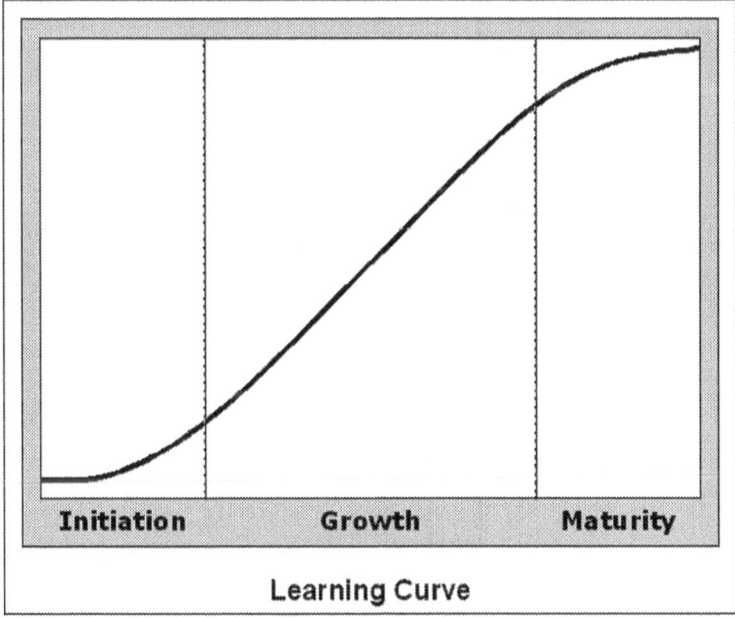

Initiation   Growth   Maturity

Learning Curve

So, don't expect to become an "expert" instantly. Consider your early attempts to be your own personal "pilot." And don't get discouraged if these early attempts don't work as well as you'd like. Keep at it. Conduct a "mental AAR." What were you trying to do? What worked? What didn't work so well? What should you do differently next time to improve results? What are the overarching lessons you need to plant in your "muscle memory?"

Phase III: Apply the GRL

The only real difference between phases two and three is your own personal confidence that the GRL really does work. After all, in Phase II "piloting" is no more than "applying," with a recognition that you may not get it "right" all the time. By phase III, you should have developed the confidence that you can successfully apply the GRL, and that it will yield the desired results. You won't have to worry, "Am I being too nice?" or "Am I giving away the store?" or, "Will the employees really respond if I allow them to make their own decisions about this or that?"

But what if you're in a situation where you're on the brink of a major change effort, and you've "made the commitment," but you haven't had time to "pilot" the GRL. What do you do? Should you plunge headlong into the project and begin applying the GRL, confident it will work? Or should you wait for the next opportunity?

My answer may surprise you. I definitely do not believe you should plunge headlong into application if you haven't had a chance to pilot. There is no way to "skip a step" in the learning process. You can't go directly from arithmetic to calculus, there are "learning" steps in between.

Nor, however, do I think you ought to just wait. The GRL is too powerful and, as is typical of human beings, our commitment probably has a half-life that's shorter than the length of the project.

No, what I think you ought to do is view the project as your practice field—your "pilot." Try some things. Take baby steps at first, but make an even more concerted attempt to learn from your early efforts. I think you'll find that the pressure of the project, combined with the energy of your commitment, will propel you up the learning curve even faster.

And, in the zeal to apply the GRL, let's not forget the other "half" of the leadership equation—the Leadership Process itself. Particularly if you're in the situation described immediately above. It turns out there may even be some serendipity that will work in your favor. One of the easiest—and perhaps one of the least risky—ways to begin to practice or apply the GRL is in the "vision" step of the leadership process.

So, in this mythical change effort that we've created, think first about where you want to go, and think about how you can truly "involve" your team in the development of that vision. And, perhaps most importantly, remember it's not enough to simply get their input and then show up at the next meeting with a completed vision. They must be active participants—not just passive recipients—of that vision. When people are treated the way they like to be treated, they respond. It's almost instinctive. They almost can't help themselves.

Phase IV: Conduct an AAR

In Phase IV, we're suggesting you go beyond brief mental AARs, as we suggested you conduct during Phase II, the GRL "pilot." Here we're suggesting that you set aside time to review your own personal application during each step of the leadership process. What did you set out to do—in terms of applying the GRL—during the vision step of the leadership process? Or the *Assemble the Team* step? And so on.

What did you actually do? Was there a difference, and why? What worked? What could be improved? What will you do differently next time? And what are the general lessons that can be applied even in upcoming steps of this same change effort?

The AAR allows us to process the experience, analyze the results, and assimilate the learnings so we can continue to improve our own performance. Without that type of review we will end up relying on our own intuition, and the weight of our past experiences may simply overwhelm our early efforts to apply the GRL.

A Closing Thought

Einstein's definition of insanity was continuing to do things the same way and expecting to get a different result. If we want a different result, we must do something different.

In this book we have endeavored to present a "new" view of leadership—a view that is actually as old as recorded history. A view that relies on people, not process, as the fundamental underpinning of effective leadership.

Now, as Edwin Markham[30] said, "We have committed the Golden Rule to memory; let us now commit it to life." Success is not a function of grand thoughts or great intentions. It is a result of action. If you have found value in this book, ideas that will enable you to make the changes in your leadership style and behaviors that you feel are appropriate, then it is now time to take action. As Oliver Wendell Holmes said, "Greatness is not in where we stand, but in what direction we are moving. We must sail sometimes with the wind and sometimes against it—but sail we must and not drift, nor lie at anchor."

We're not suggesting the path we've outlined is an easy one. But the rewards of dedication and hard work are worth the effort. Vince Lombardi echoed that thought when he commented, "Dictionary is the only place that success comes before work. Hard work is the price we must pay for success. I think you can accomplish anything if you're willing to pay the price."

And we're not suggesting that you won't experience missteps and disappointments along the way. But it's important we press on despite any discouragements we may experience. With that thought in mind, let me leave you with a perspective from Teddy Roosevelt.

It is not the critic who counts, not the man who points out how the strong man stumbled, or where the doer of deeds could have done better. The credit belongs to the man who is actually in the arena, whose face is marred by dust and sweat and blood, who strives valiantly, who errs and comes short again and again, who knows the great enthusiasms, the great devotions, and spends himself in a worthy cause, who at best knows achievement and who at the worst if he fails at least fails while daring greatly so that his place shall never be with those cold and timid souls who know neither victory nor defeat.

Notes

1   The fact that the Celtics' record during the Pitino years doesn't match his prior successes, in my opinion, in no way dilutes the key messages of Pitino's book.

2   The story of Pike Place Fish Market in Seattle has been extensively documented in a number of excellent works, including *Fish!*, by Stephen C. Lundin, Harry Paul, and John Christensen (Hyperion, New York, 2000) and *Fish! Sticks* (video by Charthouse Learning), as well as the Pike Place Fish Web site (www.pikeplacfish.com). These sources were used as reference material for the descriptions of Pike Place Fish Market and its vision.

3   Betsy Morris, "Big Blue," *Fortune Magazine*, April 14, 1997.

4   Ibid.

5   © 2003 Nantucket Group, Inc. This is a fictional case study to be used as a basis for classroom discussion only. Any similarities to real persons or places are unintentional and purely coincidental.

6   *Keep Your Eyes on the Prize*, Alice Wine, 1965.

7   U.S. television host.

8   Author and philosopher.

9   Source: ABC Television, *The Mystery of Happiness: Who has it...how to get it*, John Stossel, January 22, 1998.

10 Ibid.

11 Ibid.

12 The author is unaware of any specific attribution required for this chart.

13 Anthony J. Rucci, Steven P. Kirn, and Richard T. Quinn, "The Employee-Customer-Profit Chain at Sears," *Harvard Business Review*, January–February 1998.

14 Ibid.

15 Joint study by the Japan Human Relations Association and the National Association of Suggestion Systems in the United States (cited in *Kaizen Teian 1*, edited by the Japan Human Relations Association, Productivity Press, Cambridge, MA).

16 *40 Years, 20 Million Ideas*, Yuzo Yasudo, Productivity Press, Inc., Cambridge, MA.

17 Joint study by the Japan Human Relations Association and the National Association of Suggestion Systems in the United States (cited in *Kaizen Teian 1*, edited by the Japan Human Relations Association, Productivity Press, Cambridge, MA).

18 *40 Years, 20 Million Ideas,* Yu Yasudo, Productivity Press, Inc., Cambridge, MA.

19 The Toyota Production System and its various components have been extensively documented in a number of works including the following excellent publications: *Kanban: Just-in-Time at Toyota* (edited by the Japan Management Association); *The Machine That Changed the World* (by James P. Womack, Daniel T. Jones & Daniel Roos); and *Toyota Production System* (Toyota Motor Corporation). These sources in addition to other research (including visits to Toyota plants and discussions with Toyota management) were used as reference material for the descriptions of the Toyota Production System and its various components covered herein.

20 *Kanban: Just-in-Time at Toyota*, edited by the Japan Management Association, translated by David J. Lu, Productivity Press, Inc., Cambridge, MA.

21 James P. Womack, Daniel T. Jones, and Daniel Roos, *The Machine that Changed the World* (New York: Harper Perennial, 1991).

22 Ibid.

23 The author is unaware of any specific attribution required for this chart.

24 Eric Mann, "The Autocratic Automaker," *Multinational Monitor,* January–February, 1990.

25 Ibid.

26 The concept and methodologies of continuous improvement (or kaizen) have been extensively documented in a number of works, including *Kaizen*, Masaaki Imai, (McGraw-Hill Publishing Company, New York, NY), *Kaizen Teian I* (edited by the Japan Human Relations Association, Productivity Press, Inc., Cambridge, MA), and *Kaizen Teian 2* (edited by the Japan

Human Relations Association, Productivity Press, Inc., Cambridge, MA). These works, in addition to other research (including visits to Toyota plants and discussions with Toyota management) were used as reference material for the descriptions of kaizen as implemented at Toyota.

27 James P. Womack, Daniel T. Jones, and Daniel Roos, *The Machine that Changed the World* (New York: Harper Perennial, 1991).

28 Ibid.

29 Ibid.

30 Nineteenth-century American poet.

978-0-595-33486-5
0-595-33486-5